What We Wish Were True

What We Wish

Were True

REFLECTIONS ON NURTURING

LIFE AND FACING DEATH

Tallu Schuyler Quinn

Convergent

New York

Published in the United States by Convergent Books, an imprint
of Random House, a division of Penguin Random House LLC,
New York.

CONVERGENT BOOKS is a registered trademark and its C colophon is a
trademark of Penguin Random House LLC.

Many of the essays in this work originally appeared in slightly different form
on Tallu Schuyler Quinn's blog at www.caringbridge.org/visit/talluquinn,
in 2020 and 2021.

Additional credits for text permissions appear on page 191.

Library of Congress Cataloging-in-Publication Data
Names: Quinn, Tallu Schuyler, author.
Title: What we wish were true / Tallu Schuyler Quinn.
Description: First edition. | New York : Convergent, [2022]
Identifiers: LCCN 2021060338 (print) | LCCN 2021060339 (ebook) |
ISBN 9780593442906 (hardcover) | ISBN 9780593442913 (ebook)
Subjects: LCSH: Quinn, Tallu Schuyler—Health. | Brain—Cancer—
Patients—United States—Biography. | Women social reformers—United
States—Biography. | Women clergy—United States—Biography. |
Conduct of life.
Classification: LCC RC280.B7 Q85 2022 (print) | LCC RC280.B7 (ebook) |
DDC 616.99/4810092 [B]—dc23/eng/20220211
LC record available at https://lccn.loc.gov/2021060338
LC ebook record available at https://lccn.loc.gov/2021060339

Printed in the United States of America on acid-free paper

crownpublishing.com

2 4 6 8 9 7 5 3 1

First Edition

Book design by Fritz Metsch

To our kids, and each other

———

We become who we are together,
each needing the other. Alone is a myth.

—GUNILLA NORRIS, *Becoming Bread*

Contents

Author's Note

These days have been physically taxing, mentally confusing, and logistically full. I can't seem to get through telling even the shortest story without losing focus. I am exhausted, and my train of thought derails quickly. Comprehension of numbers, names, time, and memory are slipping at what feels like a fast clip—especially recent memories. I can communicate numbers by offering a math problem but not by saying the number itself. Anything in an order—letters, days, months—has become so disordered in my mixed-up mind. Does June come after May? My confusion is deepening. I get upside down about relationships, even my closest ones, momentarily needing to clarify that my mom is my mom and my spouse is my spouse.

But I continue to experience gratitude along this journey. It is tucked among my sorrow, my exhaustion, and my confusion. But in such a sad time, gladness takes extra effort. I hold my children close and sob when I consider what my early death will eclipse of knowing them and mothering them, and what watching me die at their young ages will mean for them. How will they experience this, tell this, live this, recover from this?

Lately I am constantly thinking about how limited our human sight is, and how "now we see in a mirror, dimly, but then face to face. Now I know in part, but then I will know fully, even as I was also fully known" (I Corinthians 13:12). What will crossing into death feel like? What does it have to offer, as I step nearer, as it pulls me in? Dying is not an experience anyone else can do for me. While others can journey closely and with profound devotion and love, no one else will be able to die for me. I'm entering that alone, even as others offer their love and presence and deep prayers for healing and peace. How unexpected that, finding myself at this threshold, I experience fullness in death and in many ways so much loss in living life.

I'm seeing we have to live with the threat or knowledge that death is imminent in order to get more honest, and I feel so much judgment in situations when I hear people complaining about their work or ranting about their spouses. And conversely, it is very difficult for me to hear my friends talk about their twentieth wedding anniversary or their children's graduation, even as I want these things for them. My mind tries to give shape to what those events and milestones will look like for my own family, our children, without me alive to be part of witnessing it all.

I am understanding that facing my own death requires an active release and deep letting go of nearly all I hold dearest. It is so, so hard, but at this threshold, I both marvel in awe and wail in despair about all the love my life contains and how those experiences of expressed love continue to be so meaningful to me. But it's in this way that profoundly, blessedly, unexpectedly, my broken heart is saving me. Decisions are clarified, relationships are repaired, attention is focused, and we are sharing more truthfully. It is not perfect, but it is courageous.

My life has been and continues to be full of extraordinary gifts:

the curved pinky fingers that look just like my dad's, the milk from my mother's chest, the profound love I feel for my two brothers, the food that sustains us, the friendships that buoy us, the trees that purify our air so we can breathe it, the animals who are slain for our nourishment, my children whose voices delight, and the body of my beloved. I am dying young of a tenacious, insidious, incurable brain cancer. But God is everywhere, for alone is a myth.

Tallu Quinn
Nashville, Tennessee
October 2021

What We Wish Were True

The Meadow

I am standing in tall grass. It is not soft. The day is overcast, but there is light, and it is slanted and bright in an almost sinister way, like rainbow weather. This meadow is where I have stood many days of my waking life. I know its soil, its roots, its curves, its weeds, its humus, its smell. And since my cancer diagnosis, I have spent nearly every day imagining myself standing here.

So many early mornings, I circled the lower acres, forging a worn path with my worries, my questions, and my footsteps. Slipping out of bed quietly so my children didn't wake, dressing in the dark and getting the buttons wrong, desperate for as many minutes to myself as I could steal. I want them back. This meadow is the place of many of my fondest memories, and now it's a place that is helping me surrender to the great beyond—that boundless dark.

One winter here my family tapped eleven sugar maples, yielding fourteen gallons of sweet sap that boiled down to only a single quart of syrup and tasted like the smoky fire upon which we cooked it. I remember our children, Lulah and Thomas, diving into the leaf piles while wearing wire butterfly wings. Lulah's wonky, early cartwheels, and Thomas's watercolor picnics. My husband, Robbie, with Lulah on his lap, waiting at the end of the driveway for me to return home from work, their faces bearing the widest smiles. The soccer ball lodged high up in the tree and how hard we laughed when our enthusiastic friends Heather and Kelsey finally kicked it out. The black walnuts we collected for dye. The hundreds of eggs the chickens gifted us in those years, and the hot breakfasts that followed. Sharing countless meals on the front porch overlooking the meadow.

And there has also been suffering here. The sixty pullets who died tragically in a coop fire while we were in Maine—the young birds charred and their wooden coop too. Our farmer friend Cari's three baby pigs she was raising attacked by coyotes in the open daylight, and countless hens picked off by predators over the years. The deep rivers of rainwater that cleaved our rocky driveway after every storm, and the literal tons of river rock we'd have hauled in to repair it. The massive pile of cleared brush and stumps, and the burns up and down our friend Sally's legs and arms when she lit it.

What is time in this meadow? Will it be my final resting place? My forever?

I keep visiting this scene in my mind—this humble place so alive with the memories of my full and happy life. Reflecting on it is helping me learn how to die. My children are there—young, bright, chubby-cheeked and glossy-chinned, smiling, taking in each other and this world we love. Does it love us back?

The grass is long. Robbie is making us laugh. No thought of my own death in the background, just the pulsing slow time of family life. With the chickens and their muck and their spilled-out food. With the tall weeds overgrown and the cardinals preening and showing themselves.

I meditate on my own death in these visits to the meadow. What will it feel like to die? Grounding myself in the memories of this place connects me to all the physical love I have encountered in this embodied life. With my eyes closed, I visualize strong tendrils shooting downward from my feet, penetrating the soil, pushing through layers of rock, and becoming roots. The roots stretch themselves through the earth's crust and arrive at the deep and strong core of all I am and have ever been and ever will be.

I come back to my breath, looping through my body as a beautiful figure eight. My mind carries me through this journey, and the present moment is full of curiosity about the unknowable past—a lineage of ancestors I never met and yet whose presence I deeply feel as I face my own death. I am carried by them, they in me, their love in me, their love is me.

Over and over again I go back to the smiling faces of my children—their grunts as they nursed at my chest, their first steps, their delight in the world around them. Our joy so big that nothing—not even death—could rob us of what we'd found and somehow formed together. I go back and I go back, and meanwhile my illness marches on, moving me forward, closer to my final days. I tell myself over and over what I have been telling my children—

Love never ends.

Angels in the Architecture

I wanted eyeglasses so badly when I was a child. Alas, I was born with excellent eyesight. I bought a pair of fake glasses from a kiosk at the old Fountain Square mall in Nashville in the third grade. One morning before school, I put them on and attempted to slip out the front door without my parents catching a glimpse of me wearing them. But my dad saw me in my fake glasses as I was darting toward the Blantons' minivan for our carpool and asked me about them. I told him I wanted to wear them to school, and he knelt down, put his hands on my shoulders, and said, "Honey, God gave you beautiful eyes and perfect eyesight, and wearing these glasses is like wearing a lie." I expertly squirmed out of his arms as quickly as I could and ran into the backyard, determined to wear the glasses. What ensued was my dad chasing me around the outside of the house to try to get them off my face. Meanwhile the Blantons were just waiting in their van watching this whole scene unfold.

Around the time I turned forty, I did pick up some readers at the drugstore because I was having trouble focusing on the computer screen and small text. These symptoms would eventually worsen a few months later, and one day I experienced a full-on inability to find and follow the cursor on my computer screen as I typed. And I noticed how I was missing whole sections of text at the end of sentences when reading to my children at night. Even connecting to a Zoom call became unusually difficult, and the reading glasses really didn't seem to help with any of this at all. I would eventually come to learn that this loss of vision was caused by an emerging cancer on the left side of my brain—specifically an area that governs vision and reading comprehension.

But prior to these visual changes, my 20/20 vision served me well. I've been thinking lately about how much of my identity has been produced by and based on being a visual person, and my creativity has especially depended on it. For as long as I can remember, I have been doing stuff with my hands—drawing, stitching, cooking, baking bread, taking photographs—making in many forms. The use of my hands paired with a strong orientation to aesthetics carried me through art school. And many a knitting project has accompanied me in countless work meetings and at conferences over the last decade. With my gaze down at the handwork on my lap, I was always telling workshop leaders, "I promise I'm listening! This knitting helps me pay attention better!" When I went into the hospital for brain surgery, I brought some embroidery to work on, anticipating a long stay. Recuperating in my post-op room, I picked it up and started to laugh hysterically with my mom because I couldn't see where to put the needle into the fabric. But I was so used to always bringing along something to do with my hands that I hadn't stopped to think about the fact that my changing eyesight might not support my hobbies anymore.

As an undergrad, I studied fiber arts, which included block and screen printing, weaving, sewing, basketry, mixing dyes, and more, each technique in its own way requiring visual decisions, math, and precision. I then became enamored with both paper-making and bookbinding. Making books and boxes requires a lot of measuring and right angles and attention to detail. The exacting nature of the field drew me in.

When I was in seminary at Columbia University in New York, I landed a work-study job in the library conserving very old books. My daily tasks were to take massive old volumes, clean them of all smudges and debris, repair torn pages with paper that matched, and then build archival boxes for them to live in. I had my little station in the archiving studio and listened to NPR on my little pocket radio all day, and the sense of accomplishment I felt using my hands was a great complement to the very heady work of deconstructing my own theological claims in the classroom.

Six months into my glioblastoma diagnosis, I discovered that a basic neurological exam always tests hand/eye coordination. So much of the satisfaction of hand/eye work is in seeing it come together, and part of being a visual person has meant I've had the kind of eyes that notice the little things. Before I got sick, if you needed something centered on a wall, or labels neatly affixed to merchandise, or leftover soup decanted into a jar for perfect yield, I was your gal! I noticed people's handwriting and fingernails and personal tics. As a child, I remember riding around in our friend Diane's Ford Taurus wagon and fixating on the way her thumbs moved over the steering wheel as she drove. I can picture my aunt Cathy's fingers poking into enriched dough as she taught me to braid bread when I was young. And even though it's been a few years since I've seen live music, my mind's eye can see our friend Fred's left hand move up and down the neck of a guitar in his seat in the round at the Bluebird Café, while the other hand expertly plays the strings.

But these days my eyesight has become more impaired, and my field of vision has dramatically narrowed. I have dense blind spots on my right side. I hit my head and bump into things and occasionally get bruises on my right arm, hip, leg, or ankle. I break mugs and cups when I'm doing the dishes because I don't see them and they fall into the sink with a crash. Recently I didn't see a lit candle on the dinner table and had a quick brush with the flame. I'll walk down the steps into the kitchen and see someone on my left. "Good morning, Dad," I'll say. Then as I scan slightly to the right, I'll say, "Oh hi, Mom!" and then look fully into the kitchen to see the rest of my family standing there, smiling and waiting to be noticed. When I went to vote, I explained to the poll worker that I needed the assistance of my spouse because of some visual impairment. She kindly handed me a form to fill out that would allow him to accompany me into the voting booth. The form's most accurate box for me essentially communicated that I am illiterate, which of course is not the case, but that is what I checked. It got Robbie and me laughing; this impairment is hard to explain!

But there are many ways of seeing, and physical sight is only one. Losing my ability to see as clearly as before, I am coming into a new understanding of my identity. There are gifts in loss, as I have been discovering and trying to share with my family and friends. And as the blind spots grow in my physical sight, what is also transpiring is a kind of removal of other blind spots that have impaired my living—perfectionism, hubris, insecurities, and more. While my eyesight is slipping away, another type of vision is emerging within. I do not believe this process is unique to me. Biblically, the theme of recovering sight to the blind is everywhere in both the Old and New Testaments, like this passage from the prophetic book of Isaiah:

And I will lead the blind in a way that they do not know,
in paths that they have not known I will guide them.
I will turn the darkness before them into light,
the rough places into level ground.
These are the things I do, and I do not forsake them. (42:16)

I believe in God's faithfulness and that God is creative and unexpected, and I believe in human resilience. As my ability to see and read has slipped away, a different kind of sight is being restored. Since I got sick, meditation and dreams and even prayers are becoming richer and easier for me to enter into and remember. Nearly every day I see faces and figures in shadows cast on walls or on pavement or in clouds. When I look out the window or along a roadside, I see faces in the winter branches. It's almost constant, and I can honestly say I am not looking for them. I think these benevolent companions—a true cloud of witnesses—have always been there, and I just couldn't see them or know them yet. It reminds me of the ethereal Paul Simon lyric: "He looks around, around, he sees angels in the architecture . . ."

It's human for us to get mired in how things used to be or what we used to be able to do but can't do anymore. For me, this visual piece of my identity is really something I grieve, and it makes me realize which of my abilities I have taken for granted. But the truth is that physical sight is only one way of knowing. I heard the legendary civil rights activist Ruby Sales talk about "complete" sight as including a mix of hindsight, foresight, and insight. To receive the gift of complete sight while lamenting what has gone away is to lean on God's covenant to liberate us from what impairs us and keeps us blind. The cancer journey is not a path I have known, and I hate it, and yet my failing eyes are opening to the gifts available to me as I walk it. Some internal sight is strengthening and lighting this darkness. And as it lights up and changes me, what I notice now is God's creative hands all over everything good, making the rough places into level ground for me, and somehow in the midst of this terror, I am not forsaken.

Ordained by Something Else

Years ago I took a workshop in which we participants were asked to create our own stoles. A stole is most commonly interpreted as a religious symbol and is typically made of fabric and worn by a minister or priest around the neck—often marking the priesthood as an identity that is set apart.

In the workshop, we were encouraged to think about "the priesthood of all believers," meaning every single one of us is called to our own work, our own vocation, and thus anyone can make use of a stole. We learned that the origin of the stole connects back to the actual use and function of a humble cloth draped around a neck to wipe a mouth, mop up a spill, bandage a wound, or dry someone's washed feet.

In a traditional ordination service, the candidate for ordination steps forward in front of his or her community and, along with their stole, receives a laying on of hands, the blessed energy flowing through from one person to another person. I believe it is a beautiful, powerful ritual for those who participate. But it typically happens inside a church sanctuary, with its white walls and sterile air, and there is no grit or grime of the very work we are most deeply called to do.

I am not ordained by the church proper, but I think about all the hands who have blessed and ordained me at my job over the years—the brilliant farmers of the refugee garden program, Judy's recipe for her mom's meatballs scribbled on a brown paper sack, David's gloved hands as he pulls in flats of berries, and Kia stitching up a wounded chicken. The thousands who have handed over delicious, nutritious meals to thousands of people in my community. The hundreds of devoted volunteers who wash lettuce, chop sweet potatoes, and fuel up the food trucks. Every one of us has hands to mend a blanket or ladle soup from a pot. There are those ordained by the community of the church and those ordained by the grit and grime of life. My laying on of hands has just been the day-to-day of ordinary work, alongside extraordinary friends, which I believe is sacred in and of itself. And we wipe those hands on the ragged and faded dishcloths from the kitchen cupboard—the stoles that mark our identities.

Cooking meals and sharing good food isn't something I do, it's at the core of who I am. Through this basic and uncomplicated work, I feel I have been pulled into the calling that is my deepest desire: God ordained and community affirmed. It's not a traditional calling, but it is an authentic one. Wiping, drying, wrapping, mopping—we toil with cloth in hand to tend and engage each other, ordained by something else.

Lemons in the Lunchbox

My surgery after my initial diagnosis went as well as could be expected. The tumor was the size of a big meaty fist. I am learning about the brain—this vital organ I know so very little about and whose enormous contributions to living I underappreciated the whole of my life. The cancer infiltrated the entire left occipital lobe of my brain, and whatever tissue that was there primarily governed vision. So what remains is just deficit.

I grieve the loss of a significant portion of my vision. It's dense loss not only of vision but of the actual part of my brain that puts letters together and processes words. With my struggle reading, I feel lucky to have a circle of readers who read to me. They read cards and emails, social media messages, even chapters of fiction and nonfiction books! My dad has been one of those readers. He has so many gifts—great storyteller, impeccable sense of humor, incredible writer. But he is a very boring reader when it comes to reading things out loud. I didn't realize this until I asked him to read me a stack of cards and letters. He sat on the edge of my bed and read to me, and eventually I said I was ready to take a nap, so he stopped. The next morning there were a few cards from the same stack that I asked Robbie to reread to me. Upon the second hearing, I bawled my eyes out at the beauty of the words and the tender correspondence and the many emotions I felt.

Almost overnight I have had to let a lot of things go. I'm not cooking as much, I can't drive any longer, my gardens are over-grown, I can't really help my kids with their schoolwork, and my own writing comes with new difficulty and requires a new effort. I used to be a compulsive list-maker. And I have dozens of journals stowed away from decades of handwritten reflections. For my early professional life, I composed sermons and other essays by typing my thoughts in chunks of text, then printing the pages and physically cutting them and rearranging the typed thoughts onto a clean, larger piece of paper. That is how visual and tactile a person I am! Eventually I reluctantly transitioned away from printed pages and learned to compose on the computer. Neither of these methods was without some struggle, but I found a competence, and I came to know that with some effort, I could write something I was proud of.

But stringing my thoughts together into written words is very difficult for me now, and I feel so much frustration with myself and my situation when I can no longer lean on my old ways of doing this thing I love. So I'm having to wrestle with words differ-ently and orient myself to a new process every few weeks, which brings with it its own annoyances but also lots of joy and laughter.

Yet I need this writing practice more than ever. The challenges of having to involve several people in this already-vulnerable pro-cess is something I am grieving exactly at the same time I feel gratitude to have those few trusted people to help me do it. Loss and gratitude go hand in hand. Writing is so much harder than ever before, and yet mercifully, writing still abides.

When I started writing long-form blog posts about my cancer, I had tools at my disposal that could help me compose on my own—my phone's accessibility features were a Godsend, and I could listen to text-to-speech, from a voice called Alicia, then dictate my words back. When I would routinely wake up in the middle of the night for a few hours, I would speak my thoughts into the phone, then have my dad proofread them and help me scrape something together. But now I can't see the phone text well enough, or follow along with words in a paragraph, to do even that.

Recently I've had trouble looking at text or images and making a simple interpretation of what I'm seeing to try to make it out. I mix up associations, getting confused about my dad's relationship to my husband or whether to cut up a lemon or an apple for my daughter's lunch. Numbers have been tricky for months, and to tell someone the number fifteen, I have to hold up a hand of five fingers and explain to them, "Three of these." When I do try to push through and get something coherent down on paper, I'm exhausted even more than usual, and I can't remember what I've written because my short-term memory is getting more limited.

It's more than just losing the ability to read, it's losing this whole dimension of how to understand myself, as an interpreter of the world, to have a chance to tell stories in a way that is really important to me. My ability to listen is a newfound grace, given that I've lost the ability to read and see. When I communicate, who knows how my words come across anymore, I can't comprehend them. But I am listening more than ever—to my own muddled thoughts, the silence of my bedroom, my daughter clanking around downstairs in the morning, and my brother's inside jokes. Sometimes I don't like being such a captive audience, but taking in what I can is my new way to thrive, and I'm all ears.

The Things They Carried

After I graduated from seminary, with a diploma in hand from a reputable institution, I did what any promising ministerial student would do: I moved to Boston with my friends and started working at a grocery store. As my former classmates accepted fabulous ministry jobs across the country, I was scheduled for the third shift at a supermarket.

I was stocking shelves, earning minimum wage, and writing the nightly restocking order for canned goods, salad dressings, oils and vinegars, dry pastas, and other shelf-stable items. My spirits were low and my limited daylight hours depressed me with a real feeling of wasting my time, with no direct application of my passion, creativity, and schooling.

Every night around 12:30 A.M., it was my job to walk through the cold cases to pull any meat with an upcoming sell-by date. I was asked to bag it up in a heavy-duty black garbage bag and chuck it into the dumpsters out back. The bags were so heavy because they were full of perfectly good meat—actual lives that had roamed this earth, now wasted—as well as all the resources that were spent raising them. There was no food donation program set up, and the sheer volume of food waste was simply baked into the economy of grocery sales. It was just business as usual. We employees couldn't even afford this food, earning the hourly wages we made.

Many years later, in my work with the Nashville Food Project, I shared this personal story with young people who were trying to find their ways in both life and career, and I told them how it's sometimes the shittiest jobs and roads to seemingly nowhere that show you a way forward and resonate with both heart and mind. One cannot always know how these difficult experiences will matter, but I feel as though my hands were being held through that time in ways that were unimaginable to me, but so crucial for giving shape to the work and perspective I would come to later.

And it wasn't the first time that I've found myself carrying something and divining meaning from it. I always seemed to be taking something along. I have carried syrup home from Maine, apples from Vermont, fish from Washington, and peanuts from Georgia. I've dragged heavy sticks up mountains, collected sharks' teeth in film canisters, kept cardboard from the streets of Harlem, and brought rocks home from every place I've ever been. I've rallied friends and family to help me move street furniture in New York, old windowpanes in Boston, a heavy metal sink in rural Tennessee, and sheets of plate glass in Kentucky.

I've sneaked honey in and out of so many countries, packed suitcases full of garden clippings for papermaking, held a sourdough starter on my lap in a moving truck, and transported thousands of leaves pressed in hundreds of books. The first Thanksgiving I was in seminary, my church hosted a big community dinner for members of our congregation and the wider neighborhood. I signed up to help serve, and after the midday meal, I asked the cooks if I could take the turkey bones home to make stock and soup. I dumped a dozen or more carcasses into a black garbage bag and asked the youth group to help me carry them uptown.

After that grocery store in Boston, I spent half a year working in Nicaragua, where I saw people carrying the most outrageous things: an eighty-year-old woman walking toward her home with a humongous pile of sticks under one arm, a long machete in the other; a young woman on the back of a motorcycle, holding a newborn baby in one arm, a five-gallon bucket of charcoal in the other. But they didn't just do it on their own, people there were always asking others to carry things too: a fifty-pound sack of mangoes for someone's mom, a skirt with seventy straight pins sticking out along the hem for someone's sister, a flannel sack of marbles for someone's cousin's son, or a box of dog medicine for someone's niece's neighbor's sick puppy.

I visited with a community in a town called Mateare, and after we finished the meeting, we packed up our truck to head back to Managua, where I was living. A woman from the community asked us if we might be able to carry her and her six children in our pickup. We said no problem, and they piled in, some in the cab and some in the back, with a really long stick in tow that they lodged into a manageable space. We were squeezed in pretty tight. A couple kilometers down the road, an old man with his thumb up asked us if we could carry him to the market in the center of Managua. We said no problem, and he piled into the back, dragging a huge black suitcase behind him. I was so uncomfortable inside the pickup, sitting backward, *on no cushion*, looking out the back window. I saw the old man unsnap the black suitcase and pull out what looked like magic tricks. He performed one for the woman and her children, and then began to juggle three balls, while he was straddling the long stick, in the moving vehicle. After the woman and her family got out and left for home, a young man with his broken-down moto asked if we'd take him to the motorcycle shop. We said yes, and he started rolling his moto toward the back of the pickup. I was thinking, *Dude, there is no way we're getting this thing in here with the big black suitcase of magic tricks, the magician, the stick, and the coolers we brought.* But we lifted his moto into the bed of the truck, and he climbed in too and somehow fit, and we drove toward town.

I thought the bag of turkey bones was the most ridiculous thing a person could carry home, but living in Nicaragua stretched my scope of our world in so many ways. The next day I got back in the same pickup truck to head to Mateare again. Twenty minutes into the drive, we stopped to pick up thirty blocks of ice, something we'd been asked to bring. I reached into the backseat for my wallet and found a real live bunny rabbit on the floor—a request from one of the community members for her farm. The bunny amazed me, kind of like a magic trick does when it works. Nicaraguan culture left me lost in translation at every turn. But if there is only one thing I understand from living there, it's that no expectation of how much I can carry or ask another to carry for me is too swollen. We brought the bunny, we made more room, we straddled the stick. We learned how to juggle, and it was magic. I mean, there are some things you just can't leave behind.

Feedback

The Gift of a Good Name

Tallu is a family name I inherited from my mom's side. It goes back many, many generations of women in our family, including my mom, Sarah Tallu. My nine-year-old daughter, Lulah, which is short for Tallulah, got the name in its fullest form. I've been told *Tallulah* is a Choctaw Indian word that means "falling waters that make people laugh." I have also heard its meaning expressed as "powerful waterfalls," and that its origin is Cherokee, not Choctaw. There is a Tallulah Falls in North Georgia, sometimes called Tallulah Gorge. When my cousin Margo and I visited there in high school with our families, the "waterfall" was more like an almost imperceptible trickle across some rocks. So powerful! Really made us laugh, though!

The layered lore of my name, including an exploration of my ancestors who held this name, is one of those things I always assumed I'd really dig into later in life.

My name is just the shorter Tallu, which has been misspelled, mispronounced, and misunderstood most days of my life. The most common and consistent (mis)pronunciation of my name has been Tally for Tallu. My last name—Schuyler—is no easier.

Often mispronounced as "Shoo-ler" or "Shy-ler," it's actually the unexpected "Sky-ler." We considered naming our son Schuyler, but so many doctors and nurses mispronounced it in the hospital during his birth that we passed it over for our other top choice, the more recognizable Thomas.

When I was in middle school, my youth group lovingly poked fun at the Tally "Shoo-ler" references by changing the words to a well-loved camp song, which includes the shouting refrain "hallelu, hallelu, hallelu, hallelujah, praise ye the lord." Instead they sang "tally-shoo, tally-shoo, tally-shoo, tally-shooler . . ." and most of them still break into song with that when they see me. Maybe it's a youth group thing?

About ten years ago I met a woman here in Nashville actually named Tally who would become one of my most treasured friends and eventually a co-worker at the Nashville Food Project. We are Tally and Tallu. One time a woman we didn't know invited Tally out to a business lunch, assuming *she* was the CEO. Tally accepted and went to the restaurant and during the entire lunch it was clear the woman thought Tally was me and the whole thing was pretty awkward and mortifying. After years of me being mistaken for a Tally, that day Tally was mistaken for me. As Tally hilariously said once, "I'm just one tiny vowel away from the big cheese."

Despite a lifetime of preemptively pronouncing my name for teachers on the first day of class, I have loved having this name. I also wonder what it will feel like to be free from it, the expectations people have of me or, more pointedly, the worldly trappings I have imposed upon myself. I hold the deepest reverence for the lineage of my maternal line, yet having the name Tallu has had the burden of being singular and strange at the same time.

The songwriter and singer Ben Harper and his mom, Ellen Harper, also a renowned folksinger and songwriter, released a record together a few years back. The whole album is beautiful, and the final song is called "How Could We Not Believe." I videoed myself trying it on the guitar during the spring that Covid-19 emerged globally. I am a real novice, and I look at the video now and I wonder if I already had a baby brain tumor in my head. In the video I sing out, "So beautiful to be free from my name . . . and all those who lay claim," while trying to get the right fingering on the strings. Who knows if it was a bit of foreshadowing, but it would be more than two months after that practice session before I would experience bad enough symptoms that would lead me to the hospital.

I am so grateful to carry on this legacy of Tallu, a heritage my daughter so proudly describes to everyone she meets. Yet as I lay claim to it in life, I anxiously wonder what the beauty of releasing it will look like.

Filling Up That Kind of Empty

When I moved to Nicaragua, it was April, and just toward the end of the dry season. I was working there as a missionary alongside farmers to alleviate food poverty in their communities. My first day on the job, I was invited to go into the *campo*, the grassy plains area, to visit a community in San Ramón de Matagalpa with my colleagues. While they were speaking with some of the community's leaders, I watched a young woman lower a plastic bucket into an almost-empty well. She held one end of a battered rope in her hands and eased the bucket down. I could hear it finding the bottom—one empty thing scraping against another—but I watched as she drew the filled-up bucket toward her body, with shaky, strong arms. She poured the water from the full bucket into an empty one beside her and carried the water out to the garden she had planted to ensure a secure source of food for herself and her family. Driving home that evening, I thought about how the fullness of their well affects the fullness of their garden which affects the fullness of their bodies, and I wondered what the community would do if the rains didn't come in soon.

Making a choice to move to Nicaragua was, in many ways, connected to my old boyfriend's love for Latin America. His dream to someday return influenced my own dream of us someday coming back together. Some dreams don't get lived the way we expect they will, and I guess that's the oldest story in the books. I arrived there soon after our breakup, and when I touched down, the emotional landscape of reasons for being there seemed pretty dry. The dream that was supposed to be fat and wet and full felt more like a tipped-over bucket, with my hopes spilled out everywhere in Spanish and other stuff I didn't understand. In a million nameable ways, the bucket of being there felt like that dream dried up.

Many people in the world spend whole days in the work of moving water from full places to empty ones, using buckets and bowls and hands. This daily work often ensures that there will be water for the next meal, the next day, the next need. I lived in a house with a lot of water issues—the pipes were dry, the pipes were leaking, the faucet was broken, or the water was not potable. When the water did run, the family I lived with saved it for the next time there would be none. This usually involved moving around a dozen oddly shaped plastic buckets with ill-fitting lids, and stacking them for various needs—washing, drinking, flushing, cooling down. A hundred times I went to the pipe for water and there was none, and I learned how to move the water from where it was to where it wasn't.

Exactly what I expected would be so full was so empty: the faucet was dry, and it often didn't rain for so many days. But the rainy season had just started, and the water began slowly coming in. I liked to imagine the well in San Ramón getting fuller every day, and their gardens growing fat and green. And as time passed, I had to believe my own water lines would rise too and that a new dream could grow inside the shell of an old one. While I waited for the water to fill in, I tried to move the buckets around in a pattern all my own—lowering down into what felt empty and trying to love up what I found there. And maybe one day I will find myself fat and full from swallowing down this kind of empty.

Up Here on the Shore

During this last year and a half of having glioblastoma, I've been learning how much I can do in a day, which is much less than I used to do, but it's still a whole lot, and I feel a deep, deep sense of gratitude for that. I take naps most days and build fires in our fire pit and walk into Green Hills to get groceries and make dinner most nights. There is so much I can't do and so much out of my control, so I've noticed how much I'm drawn to tasks I can control around the house—purging closets, taking art to be framed, going through boxes of photos, picking up kindling in the yard, and even ironing linen napkins! Until then, I hadn't ironed anything in two decades! All this is to say, Reinhold Niebuhr's profound Serenity Prayer has never resonated in a more obvious and helpful way.

Maybe death is not the worst thing? My wise friend James offered this thought in conversation a few months back. He wasn't exactly saying it to me, but to both of us, as something to consider and reflect on. I remember wanting to be brave enough to believe it, and I've thought about the question most days since. With the tragic number of Covid deaths in the last two years, death and dying are in the collective ether. And for me, my family, and our community, questions and fears about death are constant. As I fold the laundry and organize the Tupperware, I have been reflecting on James's thought—maybe death really isn't the worst thing?

But if it's not, then what is? As I continue to ponder it, I keep coming back to the different ways our modern culture fails to embrace life and all its joys. Perhaps the worst thing is not death but the ways we cover up our own desire to express deep reverence for life. We enslave ourselves to work, to our screens, to distraction and denial—all forms of oppression. We chain ourselves to power and wealth and comparison and measuring up to someone else's ideas of who we ought to be. We covet their opinions of us. We stay small. We dull the shine, dim the inner light. We armor up our vulnerabilities and use our coldness as weaponry. We want to see people for who we want them to be instead of who they are. We mute the gifts of others. Some of us barely scrape together enough calories from ketchup packets, while others of us scrape full meals off our plates into the garbage disposal. We extract and privately own what is not ours. We appropriate and exploit. We do not face and admit to the violent and racist beginnings of our nation, the legacies of which persist into the present day and live in me. I have been complicit in all this. I have provoked this pain, been complacent to this pain, suffered at the hands of this pain. And our collective pain gets so lodged in us that we become incapable of praise and joy, and we pass on our hurts to our children, and the cyclical nature of generational pain continues.

Culturally, we do not make a lot of room to grieve. We gloss over the depths of others' sorrow or even our own. We move on, we say nothing. Out of respect, we do not name the pain, and the great irony is that a failure to name it keeps the hurting one in a state of hurt.

I remember meeting over lunch with my friend Sarah in New York years ago, when I was going through a very difficult time after my cousin Beth died by suicide. I felt so close to Beth, and yet how did I not know she was suffering so deeply? I think Sarah picked up on a lot of self-judgment for what I was feeling about Beth at that time, and said, "Tallu, feelings just are; they're not good or bad, they just are." That had never, ever occurred to me!

This aversion to embracing or sharing our true feelings swings in both directions. It's difficult to express not only deep sadness in grief but also praise and love and desire. The vulnerability required is enormous. Perhaps failure to grieve is connected to cultural influences not to embrace life. I've been listening to a book my friend Brooke recommended called *The Smell of Rain on Dust: Grief and Praise* by Martín Prechtel. He narrates it, and I love the cadence and sound of his voice. The core theme is that grief is always linked with praise—necessarily—and we have a cultural aversion to grieving because we do not know how to adequately praise the miracles of life all around us.

So maybe death is not the worst, but becoming so numb that we don't even grieve our losses is. And loss is of course not always death, but includes any experience when someone or something we want disappears or goes away. I am learning now that grieving is an obligation. When our sadness is not properly processed in grief, it shows up as anger and violence toward self and others, as depression, as abuse, and as constant dissatisfaction. When we don't do our own grieving, we burden someone else with it.

So how do we grieve well? I guess the only way out is through. I am learning that grief is active, not a static state of sadness or sorrow to stay in. What does active grieving look like? Years ago I got to have tea with my friend Holly at the Café at Thistle Farms. She talked with this light in her eyes about her incredible daughter

Lauren who had died years before. So vulnerably, she shared with me the work she did to grieve her daughter's tragic death. I was in awe of her bravery and acceptance of what had come to be and how actively she embraced a process of grieving. It still moves me to think about this.

Another inspiration has been Sheryl Sandberg's account of her process of grieving after her husband, Dave, died unexpectedly when they were on vacation. She humbly and vulnerably shares her story in an interview on NPR's show *On Being* and speaks specifically to some of the Jewish rituals around grieving that helped her and her children in the wake of his death.

And after one of my miscarriages our friend Courtney sent us a gorgeous book called *Tear Soup* that is phenomenal for explaining how grief is active and for affirming that everyone has a different way of grieving loss. It's not important to do it a specific way but one's own way.

Deeply grieving my death is the obligation I have to this life I love. I will not shrink from the sadness I feel, but neither will I quit my imperfect praise. I crashed into life like a wave, and like all waves I will return to my source, the bigger body of life from which I was made. I do not know when the final pull and recede will happen, but it will for me and it will for you. Have I done all I was meant to do up here on the shore? Have I paid good attention? Did I adequately praise all there is to love here?

A Sleepy Loop

In Nicaragua, every weekday, I took a morning walk with a bunch of the people I lived with. I would wake up at 4:55 for a five A.M. departure—just enough time to get dressed and put on my shoes. If I woke up even five minutes earlier, I think I would have had time to convince myself to sleep instead of walk, which is, of course, exactly what I would have done. But once I was on the walk, I was more or less glad to be moving, and I'd start to wake up. As we went along, we gathered little pieces of information about our neighborhood and our neighbors: who was dumping their garbage into the stream that goes to the lake, and who was lighting theirs on fire; who was drunk and strolling home at such a late (early) hour; who hadn't cleaned the dog-doo off their stoop.

One week we saw the man who lived across the street kissing his next-door neighbor's maid goodbye at five in the morning. The week before, we huddled around a hole where a lime sapling had been pulled up and stolen at some point in the night. And the week before that, we were only thirty-five minutes late to a minor crime scene, and a pool of the perpetrator's blood was spilled fresh on the sidewalk as proof. We saw shirtless men in their house shoes and old women wearing thin nightgowns. We saw bony dogs with pink skin, long tits, and dried scabs. We saw drug deals on the footbridge and tiny gorgeous children getting dressed for school. We saw men squatting on corners with emptied bottles of rum, and we saw the light of television sets inside every home. We saw *tortillerías* opening up, the men working the coals and the women working the masa. We saw neighbors sweeping up yards of dirt and hosing down dusty sidewalks. It was our version of the *Today* show that unfolded in real time, where we took the pulse of how the night had passed and how the day before us might unfold. It was weather, it was local news, it was how we opened up our day—just a long and sleepy loop around the block.

Knowing What You Want

In late summer of my six months in Nicaragua, I got a call from my childhood friend Clay. He reached out with a job opportunity at my home church in Nashville, where he had recently been called to serve as senior minister. A local arm of an Austin, Texas–based nonprofit called Mobile Loaves and Fishes had been operating in Nashville and had moved to Woodmont Christian Church's campus, to the very building where I had attended Sunday school growing up. Mobile Loaves engaged volunteers to prepare sack-lunch-type meals and share them from food trucks in poor neighborhoods throughout Nashville—tent cities, apartment complexes, daily-rate motels, housing projects, and for people living unhoused and on the streets.

Honestly, I never thought I'd return to the city where I grew up, much less to the very church where I had been raised. But that was the invitation in front of me. The part-time program manager of the nonprofit had recently put her notice in, and the ministry was looking to replace her. Clay asked whether I had any interest in speaking with those overseeing the hire, and I said yes. I Skyped an interview with four strangers who would become dear to me—Rob, Berry,

Bill, and Gordon—a de facto advisory board for Mobile Loaves and Fishes in Nashville. They hired me for twenty hours a week to oversee the food truck program and move it forward. Alongside this, Woodmont offered me another part-time role on its ministerial staff, and these two jobs were my work path back to Nashville.

While the food was a crucial component of the help that Mobile Loaves offered in and around Nashville, relationships also formed out of the organic moments that the help generated. And eventually these conversations with volunteers and community members led everyone involved to consider big ideas. Fundamentally the sack lunches we offered from the food truck helped those who were stretched to find employment, housing, and food, because it allowed them to focus on stable employment or housing without having to worry about long-term hunger. But this work was a Band-Aid for the wider dilemma of poverty, and it begged questions about whether we were doing more harm through one-time aid than good.

After accepting the job and booking my flight home to Nashville, I remember making long lists of what this food-focused ministry could become, potentially incorporating educational and employment opportunities, communal kitchens, food gardens, and more. With love and affirmation and some caution, my mom suggested it would take ten years to accomplish all the ideas I was putting down into the pages of my sketchbook. I felt frustrated by the thought of waiting ten years to realize these dreams, but dang, she was right.

My closest expat friend in Nicaragua, Patty, pored over my sketchbooks with me and said, "T, it's so powerful to know what you want in life, isn't it?" And soon after I got back to the states, Patty came to Nashville for a visit. One early morning we were sitting in the car, and I told her more about my new job and the feeding program that I'd just started supporting. She said, "T, why do you call it a feeding program? The way you say that makes it sound like you're feeding cattle."

"What would be another name for it?"

"I don't know, maybe a food project or something like that?"

And so it would come to be—in the fall of 2011, just two years after my return from Nicaragua, we would transform the existing Mobile Loaves and Fishes on Woodmont Christian's campus into an independent nonprofit called the Nashville Food Project. It was a scrappy start-up that was full of passion but miles from the justice-based, community-food work we ultimately wanted to be doing. But that would come in time, by incorporating the gifts of so very many who were, at that juncture, still unknown to us.

And Patty was right, it's so powerful to know what you want in life. I began in earnest to meet people in Nashville with a shared desire to support antipoverty work from a justice-based lens and a focus on recovering, growing, and cooking healthy, nourishing food. A small poster hanging in my office proclaimed, "Nothing about us, without us, can be for us." This profound statement went against everything I'd been steeped in growing up in Christian charity work, and it would be an uphill climb in learning how to unwind from the approach of doing "for" instead of doing "with." But I wanted it so bad, and I could see the potential in ways that galvanized.

But there were also days that paralyzed. I believe that is the nature of any start-up, or any ministry work at all. But we kept going.

A lot of people over the years have expressed how much Nashville needed the Nashville Food Project. And I believe them. What I have felt, wrestled with, and gratefully come to also believe is how much I needed the Nashville Food Project, too. For years, I was wrestling with God and with myself about my purpose and place and role, and here it was before me all the while—the mission we keep folding ourselves into, which I've come to understand as the perfect recipe: to grow, to cook, and most important, to share. The Nashville Food Project is not a church, but it is a community that saves people. It saved me.

So What

When I received my terminal cancer diagnosis, I knew I would have to leave my job in a daily way. The night I found out I had a brain tumor, I texted Susannah from the emergency department with the news. Susannah was not only a dear friend but my board chair at the time. I texted, "We are going to need a new CEO," and she wrote back, "I understand," and with immense gratitude, I surrendered and turned the whole thing over to her. And that was it. Even though I felt the shock of that quick decision, it wasn't the first time I'd engaged with the question to quit. Over the last twelve years, I've turned in at least two formal resignation letters to my board and written another dozen in my mind. Each time I was lovingly convinced to stay, as the founder and CEO of something that had started for me in the drab rooms of a church outbuilding.

The desire to unwind from my role seemed to emerge in moments of acute burnout, or paradoxically, in seasons when there was obvious stability within the organization, times when I told myself I could responsibly leave. The prompting to step down tended to be personal, like when we started growing our family, or professional, when I knew I could walk away without saddling the next leader with a mess. I was keenly aware that there's often an expiration date on when a founder's influence continues to be beneficial. I could see how the strengths of the organization reflected my own strengths, and similarly, its short-comings reflected my own shortcomings. I had a sense that the longer I stayed, the harder it would be for someone else to take over. Or would it just be harder for me to go?

But when I got the text back from Susannah, the questions of when and how to leave were answered. The reasons couldn't be disputed or reconsidered. It was just this true and devastating blow both to me personally and to the organization at large. It had taken me more than two decades to find and claim my path, and then, just as I felt I was finding sure footing walking it, I had to give it up in one night.

Twenty years earlier I could never have guessed I would be facing such decisions. I was nearing graduation from seminary and working several jobs. One of them was doing some chef work for a couple of affluent families on the Upper West Side of New York City. One afternoon in the last semester of school, my professor and mentor, Janet, came over for a meal in my tiny New York apartment. We sat down together at the table where we had big green salads that I'd made for our lunch. She said to me, "So what are you going to do?"

With graduation less than a month away, I understood her question to be an inquiry into my plans for the immediate future. "Well, I'm doing some private chef work for a couple of families here in New York, which is pretty lucrative, so I'll probably stay in the city and continue." And before I could finish, she squarely put her hand down on the table between our salads and said, "No, Tallu, what are you going to do about poverty?" At school, along-side my classes, my most influential encounters were in small church kitchens in my role as the cook for a program called the Poverty Initiative, now an anchor of the Poor People's Campaign. The Poverty Initiative hadn't had a cook before, but seeing the money the organization was spending on food ordered in—like shitty fruit trays and sugar-laden doughnuts—I volunteered to help with catering support for our New York meetings and events.

My work blossomed as I got to know people within the Poverty Initiative, and they got to know me. What emerged in those friendships was full of possibility, and those possibilities took off. Our work was centered out of New York, but the larger movement spanned the entire United States, and we seminary students had the opportunity to enroll in immersive trips to other cities where we met with organizers in different parts of the country. We students were invited to listen to their stories, engage in their local campaigns, reflect on what role religious communities had to play in shifting from charity work to justice-based work, and raise up religious leaders to carry that work forward.

Cooking allowed me to get out of my head during grad school, which is sadly where too much theological reflection resides, and to wrestle with the plaguing realities of economic injustice, environmental degradation, systemic racism, low wages, and more. It was a crucial pairing with the more formal academic aspects of my theological education in the classroom. The people and experiences were as important as any text I read or paper I penned.

My travels with the Poverty Initiative took me to the Mississippi Delta, Memphis, New Orleans, and all through Appalachia, including West Virginia, Tennessee, and Kentucky. We visited Ithaca, Rochester, and all across upstate New York. On these work trips, my task was to cook two to three meals a day for movement leaders and the seminary students who accompanied them. My friend Paul and I, and anyone else we could pull into our joyous daily grind, would set up in church kitchens in each town, take inventory of what equipment onsite we had to work with—often very little—plan menus, shop for food during the day, and cook a big meal for each night's dinner. Walking the aisles of the small-town grocery stores provided a striking snapshot of the realities local people faced in accessing nutritious food. We did anything we could to funnel our modest budget and buying power into these local places, and we tried our hardest to find the best meat, the freshest vegetables, and loaves of decent bread.

During the days we engaged students with a wide range of kitchen skills to wash greens, chop produce, whisk up big batches of marinades, bake muffins by the dozens, and pull together "compost cookies" with whatever nuts and dried fruit and nibs of chocolate we could find. We braised chicken thighs with olives and dried fruit, spun romaine for Caesar salad for 120 people, and added unsweetened cocoa powder to large pots of chili to punch it up before asking the room of eaters that night to guess its secret ingredient. We brewed up simple salty broths for everyone after a long day in the January cold. There would be nut-studded muffins and egg stratas for the next morning alongside hot coffee, and always something thoughtful and delicious for the vegetarians. I knew the work, I loved the work, and I loved the compliments. The daily planning and daily grind were incredible preparation for what would come years later in the Nashville Food Project kitchens.

As I observed my fellow students preaching, writing, reporting, documenting with various media, and more, I found my best role to be supporting them as their cook. I'd watch them give impassioned speeches and speak truth to power and compare myself to them; I just never felt like I could do those things well and authentically. I told myself the story that I didn't have the gifts to be a pastor of a church and didn't have the smarts to be an academic. But the humble, often hidden work of a kitchen I knew, and I settled into the idea that it could be my way of meaningfully contributing to something just and good in our broken world.

The leaders of our organization were poor people with agency and power. Growing up privileged and steeped in charity-laden Christianity, I hadn't had the experience of being part of communities where poor people had been leaders or had voice or had been honestly recognized for anything other than their deficiencies and needs. It changed my life to drink coffee after dinner with men and women who had lived poor most of their lives. Up until these encounters, I didn't personally know any poor people. Why? This question of why would be one I'd continue to pull forward in my religious and professional life.

One mark of a good mentor is someone who can call you out on your bullshit, while simultaneously offering up their constant encouragement and support. Janet, and her challenge to me right before graduation, did that for me. I remember another time she and I were in a basement in Mississippi somewhere, after dinner, nearing the end of an immersive trip through the region of the Mississippi Delta. Janet encouraged me to let in the problems of the world enough not to paralyze me but to galvanize me to do more. As I made my way through the ensuing years, I would think about these two words so often—*paralyze* and *galvanize*—their strong and opposing forces, and the space between them.

Becoming Bread

We are all mere beggars telling
other beggars where we found bread.
—MARTIN LUTHER

It seems like the minute I got sick, all these photographs of me holding loaves of bread showed up on the Internet—like dozens of them! I actually love this and think about bread as a symbol threading through my adult life. A few years ago I had the pleasure of being part of a twelve-person spiritual formation group at my church. At the conclusion of our year together, we went on a retreat, and there was a session called Give God Words during which our facilitators Dana and Steve offered each participant a small frame with a single personalized God-word inside. The God-word I was given was *bread* (in Harry Potter font), and the members of our group commented that I offered bread in so many forms to so many, and that this bread was both actual and spiritual food. My framed God-word generously gifted to me sits on our bathroom shelf, where it offers me a little lift and nourishment each morning. Give me this day! My daily bread.

The loaves of bread in the photographs of me are not props. I have been learning to bake bread for the last thirty years, and I most earnestly (albeit clumsily) devoted myself to it when my friend Kate gave me a Martha Rose Shulman bread book for my sixteenth birthday. I can remember our attempts at bagels and boiling them in a stockpot before baking, as well as practicing an herbed country loaf I still love to bake today.

At this point, my approach to bread baking is a combination of many recipes I've encountered since then. I like the addition of malt powder for baguettes, something I gleaned from *America's Test Kitchen* to boost both flavor and color. I like baking in a Dutch oven and adding water to a pan on the lower rack for a good lift in the loaf. I picked up a technique of turning the bread dough using a very wet hand, a trick offered in the *Artisan Bread in Five Minutes a Day* book. But all I am is just a home baker, with an absolute devotion to the most wonderfully nourishing food of all—bread. In addition to making it, I love to find good loaves everywhere I can, and I have carried bread home from San Francisco (Tartine), Louisville (Blue Dog), Boston (Clear Flour), Santa Fe (Sage), and of course, my favorite right here in Nashville: Dozen Bakery.

A month or so before the Covid-19 pandemic hit, I taught a breadmaking class at my friends Katy and Dave's house. In preparation, I wanted to have a large amount of bread dough ready to shape and bake off, along with plenty of ingredients to make a fresh batch of dough for the participants to take home with them. I had an enormous bin of all-purpose flour in our minivan, and I can't remember how it happened, but flour ended up all over the dark interior of my car. It was an unbelievable amount of white powder in every crevice and on every surface. And some water spilled, at which point the inside of our minivan started to smell like dough and fermentation. It was a totally overwhelming amount of flour, and I wish another person had been with me to hear the line of questioning I got at the auto wash when I went to have it detailed: "Um, ma'am, what is the nature of this white powdery substance?"

When I was attending Union Theological Seminary, the brilliant songwriter John Bell from the Iona Community in Scotland spent a week there as an artist-in-residence. He's penned some of my favorite modern hymns, and during his visit to New York he wrote music with our community, led worship, and taught us students how to lead worship, too. One night during his stay, I had the chance to host him and a few students in my apartment. At the time, a no-knead bread recipe perfected by the baker Jim Lahey was all the rage—his technique had recently been published in *The New York Times*. It relies on a very long proof and results in a very wet dough. Since I was hosting this group, I decided to go ahead and bake an experimental loaf of crusty bread with my dough that had been rising, but it was so wet that it spread out and flattened itself along the bottom of my large, oval-shaped Dutch oven, and it came out of the oven wide and flat. But to this day, it had the best crumb of any bread I've baked! I kept disparaging the flatness of the loaf as we tore into it, but it was John who complimented it and turned the evening into communion.

Years ago in a Jewish shabbat service I attended, there was a lacquered loaf of challah on a table with a beautiful embroidered cloth on top. Before we shared the bread, Rabbi Rami Shapiro referred to the cloth covering the loaf as he removed it and prayed over it and said, "Imagine . . . if this is the care with which we treat the bread, then imagine the care with which we are asked to treat one another." My friend Viki comes to mind when I consider this responsibility to care for one another. She has been bringing us her homemade bread most weeks since we learned of my diagnosis—either three loaves of ciabatta or one larger crusty boule. And it was Viki who actually taught me that the word *accompany* has origins in French and Latin that mean "to come with bread" or "to be a bread friend." I guess *accompany* is her God-word, which is bread by another name.

I've noticed the connections between the biblical words *took, blessed,* and *gave.* These three verbs appear in the gospel story known as "feeding the five thousand" and then again later at the Last Supper—*take and eat, this is my body which is given for you.* In my living, I have hitched myself to this nourishment. I have devoured it, botched it, buttered it, forgotten to salt it, burned it, and relished it. I have tried to take, bless, and give. I have not always lived into that call and have certainly eaten more than my fair share. On a recent phone call, I asked my friend and former co-worker Emily if she would make bread for all who attend my funeral. I imagine long tables and thick pieces of bread on big platters, and little bowls tucked among the platters holding the best butter, honey, and—if it's in season when I die—this citrus jam from Costco that I love. All these years I have been working out my own ways to come with bread for others and for myself, and I guess in my death, I hope to go out with bread too.

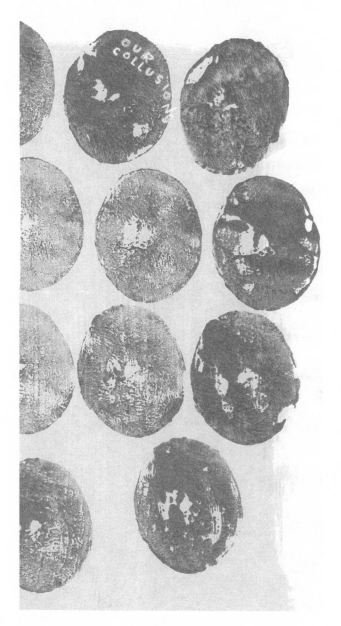

imaging

Cinnamon Soup

My parents didn't let my brothers and me buy a lot of stuff when we were kids, but they would pretty much always say yes if it was a book we were asking for. I remember finding this cookbook on the shelf of the Moravian Book Shop in Bethlehem, Pennsylvania, my dad's hometown, sometime in the late eighties. The Moravian Book Shop was one of those independent bookstores that was under threat of going away when the big chain stores came on the scene, but thankfully it continues to thrive today. My devout grandmother Vivian worried sick when the bookstore abandoned their policy of being closed on Sundays so they could compete with other retail. She thought the world was coming to an end!

Anyway, my dad and I bought this cookbook there, and he promised me we could cook the recipes together. It was written by the comedian and actor Dom DeLuise. I was maybe eight or nine, and because of the cookbook, I thought he was a chef, but I understand now he was mainly a larger-than-life comic actor, an unlikely celebrity author for what I thought was an elite gourmet cookbook. I fondly recall making the marinara sauce recipe with my dad in our kitchen at home. Tomato splattered everywhere—what a mess we made.

I just always seemed to be finding food, or food was finding me. Growing up, I loved food shows like *The Frugal Gourmet* and Julia Child's *The French Chef*, and any other food show on television. I vividly remember an episode of *Mister Rogers' Neighborhood* when he visited a Pittsburgh bakery and learned how to make sourdough pretzels. Later on in life, I loved Food Network shows like *Molto Mario*, *Nigella Feasts*, and *Barefoot Contessa*. I am proud my two children love watching *The Mind of a Chef*, *America's Test Kitchen*, and *The Great British Baking Show*. When my son is reaching that point during bedtime where he's worn out and falling apart, he'll often ask to sit with me and watch an *America's Test*, and we'll get in bed and watch Julia and Bridget baste a fish or Adam review apple corers.

And both kids, like me, have a way of imposing their will and experimenting with their own independence in the kitchen. When Thomas was five, taking after his eager older sister, he started making cinnamon soup (usually a tepid bowl of water with cinnamon floating on top), but the fallout of cinnamon scattered around the kitchen, and the cost of constantly replacing our herbs and spices, took a toll. I wonder how the kids pursued these notions so strongly, but then I remember when I was really young and my grandmother was visiting us from Pennsylvania. One afternoon I reached into the fridge for the gallon jug of milk to pour a glass. Grammy said, "You're going to spill that," and I said, "No I won't—I do this all the time," so indignant that she thought I was too little to pour it on my own. I grabbed the gallon jug, started pouring the milk, and Grammy said to me again, "You're going to spill, you're going to spill," and then I did. I spilled the milk everywhere.

A real turning point in my coming not just into a keen interest in food but into a real knack for making it was learning how to prepare, in earnest, a proper roast chicken. It was early in college, when I was learning papermaking at the Appalachian Center for Craft, and I was living on my own for the first time. I started cooking for myself and asking my teachers and older students about any cooking they did. Now when I think about cooking a bird or cooking a chicken, it's no big deal, I don't even think about it as a recipe, but at the time I remember having to follow all the steps of how to do it—reading each section of the recipe and following it to a *T*. How to turn a bird into something you could eat and want to eat—it seems so simple ultimately, but it's also so fundamental. I had a sense through all my trials and errors that it was a crucial part of a chef's toolbelt. If you can learn how to prepare a roast chicken, you can do a lot of things. And after a while, I started going off script. I usually first rinsed and patted down the whole bird, then I began to experiment, layering soft, herbed butter beneath loosened skin. After I settled into my own recipe for chicken, it was on to other dishes. How to make salad dressing. How to prepare fresh radishes for a dinner platter. And so on.

And even though I was still learning, I don't think I gave up my eagerness or big-brush vision at all. In celebration of my parents' twentieth wedding anniversary, I made crab cakes with aioli—a recipe lifted from a *Food and Wine* cookbook that was likely, to this day, the most elaborate recipe I ever attempted. I set a table on our covered stone porch and laid the crab cakes on it like a masterpiece. In the kitchen at my parents' house, much as in the ordeal of Dom DeLuise's marinara sauce, no spoon, no measuring instrument, no bowl went unused. I don't remember if anybody at the anniversary dinner ate the crab cakes. And I don't know if Thomas really knows whether we eat his cinnamon soup every time he concocts it. But food has always been the medium in every house where I've lived, without a doubt.

Leftover Spaghetti

Sometimes when I talk with young people, I ask them to remember a time that really burned them up, a time they encountered a situation that was just wrong to the core. These are the moments, one hopes, that become catalysts for action rather than apathy. A Poverty Initiative trip through Louisiana and Mississippi after Hurricane Katrina held several of those moments for me personally. The injustice and tragedies that Katrina left in its wake were not hard to see or identify. I remember the days we spent in Biloxi, Mississippi. The town was ravaged by a storm surge after the hurricane. In our cleanup efforts, we were asked never to open freezers or refrigerators. I spent an eight-hour day recovering family photographs on a cleanup site. It felt like pissing in the wind, the devastation so much larger and more encompassing than this one family's wasted front yard. How could my tiny contribution possibly be meaningful in the wake of such enormous loss? One of the stark realities of that visit was seeing up close how a town could lay devastated, but the casinos offshore were up and running, humming along, all their glory and function fully returned. One of the Biloxi residents we met told us that the only place to get their FEMA checks cashed was at the open casino on the water. I was outraged to learn that something established to be crucial and helpful was actually setting vulnerable people up for failure, especially during a relief effort for a disaster that left everything hanging by threads.

I was paralyzed by the scope of injustices like these, yet galvanized by the good work I saw supporting positive change in communities in small but meaningful ways. I was trying to figure out how to turn experiences like the ones I had in Biloxi into a vocational path forward. Food was my passion, social justice felt like my responsibility, and ministry seemed like my communal calling. Deep down I wanted to be a minister, and knew deep down that I couldn't be anything else—that it was deeply, profoundly my call to share the hope I carried. But in my late twenties, ordination into a single denomination felt too narrow. I could not authentically and wholly commit myself to the church the way ordination asked me to, and so I claimed a place ever-so-slightly outside of it.

Food had become a way to engage with antipoverty work, but it was incomplete on its own. Justice work was inspiring, but I needed to find a place to focus it. And the idea of church-based work had me clinging to the possibility and even audacious promise of repair and healing that I found in the gospel stories. Each pursuit lent something crucial to the efficacy of the other. Pursuing any one of them alone seemed insufficient and too limited. My desire was to find and walk a path that engaged social justice, real food, and liberation theology, but there wasn't an obvious single organization that was blending these three strong vocations together. I didn't see anyone else doing it in the interconnected ways I believed were possible.

Father James Martin, S.J., a Jesuit priest and author, tells a story about being called to the priesthood while eating a bowl of leftover spaghetti alone and watching a documentary on PBS. After this experience, he left his job in finance to follow a call to ministry. In his writing he speaks specifically to how God calls us through our desire. We are all called to be the person God made us to be; this is not limited to one's job but the whole of one's life. At that time in my life, I was looking for a way to pull together my desire into meaningful work. It strikes me now what a privilege it was and is to even consider one's desire and one's dreams in the pursuit of one's job. How grateful I am that many along the way encouraged me to use my outrage to seek a vocational path, especially an unlikely one.

A Little More Time

Another morning and I wake with thirst
for the goodness I do not have. I walk
out to the pond and all the way God has
given us such beautiful lessons. Oh Lord,
I was never a quick scholar but sulked
and hunched over my books past the hour
and the bell; grant me, in your mercy,
a little more time. Love for the earth
and love for you are having such a long
conversation in my heart. Who knows what
will finally happen or where I will be sent,
yet already I have given a great many things
away, expecting to be told to pack nothing,
except the prayers which, with this thirst,
I am slowly learning.

—MARY OLIVER, "Thirst"

I nursed my babies long and late, especially my son, Thomas. Just before his fourth birthday, we visited my parents at Jekyll Island, Georgia, where we planned to leave him, along with his older sis-

ter, for a week to finally wean. Robbie and I flew back to Nashville, and the first night Thomas woke up in my parents' bed and
asked to nurse. My mom told him, "I'm sorry, but that's the one
thing I can't do. Is there something else you might want for comfort?" He said, "Do you have any chips?" And they sat up and ate
chips in bed for a while before going back to sleep.

I am gripped by the likelihood that I will die young and my
children will probably not remember me. There will be photographs and stories, and many people to tell them, about the person
I was and the life I tried to live. I have even thought about how
some people will tell my kids I was amazing, and how I don't even
want that to be the story they hear. I don't want to be immortal-
ized on a pedestal in my death, I just want to stay alive for as long
as I can as the flawed still-alive human I am. I want to own my
mistakes and show my kids how to apologize. I have been thinking
so much about my limitations as a mother. A year or two ago I
heard the poet Sharon Olds speak about parenthood in an interview, commenting, as she entered motherhood, that of course she
wouldn't be making the same mistakes that her own parents had
made in raising her, but then she paused and said, "But I didn't
realize how many other mistakes would be available to me!"[1]

Last summer I sat with Stephen over lunch at my work. We are
old friends with a special connection and were just catching up. I
don't remember how we got there in our conversation, but we
talked about his own mother's death when we were teenagers, and
how unfair it was that his mom didn't get to see the extraordinary
adult he had become or know the family he would make with his
wife, Malinda, and how everyone needs their mom for as long as
possible. During my long cancer journey, my own mom has held
my hand to cross the street, changed my sheets, driven me to

appointments, cried with me, made me laugh so hard I couldn't breathe, and so much more.

So I'm feeling pretty sad for myself and my kids lately. I guess there are going to be a lot of days like this. Unimaginable suffering and deep love are two sides of the same coin. I don't want to pack nothing. I want to hold on to it all.

The Owl and the Pussycat

To celebrate our ten-year wedding anniversary, Robbie and I took a trip to Black Mountain, North Carolina. The minute I climbed into the passenger seat of our minivan and clicked on my seatbelt to ride east with him, I burst into tears. We had just come from Thomas's kindergarten graduation, and I could not stop crying. The weeks before had been full of complicated logistics and tons of communication and doctors' appointments, and finally slowing to a near-stop in the moving car drummed up so many feelings of profound love for my family, as well as heartbreak about my cancer marching forward faster than I imagined. Everything brings tears lately—the smell of my children's skin, the sounds of their voices, their loose teeth, and even their lost shoes that we frustratingly can't ever seem to find in the mornings.

I feel so much gratitude for Robbie these days. He handles the driving, the finances, the childcare, the reading, the big decisions, the large medicine planner, and more. As he and I reflected this weekend on our married years, we laughed at how the origin of our initial dates is kind of storied. Thirteen years ago, while I was still working in Nicaragua, we had been exchanging letters—real snail mail! When I got back home to Nashville, I reached out to him to see if he wanted to get together. After several weeks of hoping I'd hear from him, I heard nothing. Radio silence, circa late summer 2009. I was so confused and disappointed after receiving such sweet correspondence in Nicaragua. Finally one night I called him, and he answered the phone. He was confused and thought I was calling from Atlanta, a notion that made me even more confused.

About twenty minutes later, I got an email with a copy of a text exchange between him and his younger brother Andrew. I had just bought a new phone stateside and gotten a new number, which happened to be nearly identical to Andrew's. Robbie had just gotten a new phone too and had been texting Andrew for more than a week, thinking he was texting me! We have these texts, which were read at our rehearsal dinner and then again at Andrew's rehearsal dinner years later, to prove it.

Our wedding itself is storied. It spanned a full and dreamy long weekend at our beloved church camp, Bethany Hills. We roasted pigs, slept in bunk beds, and welcomed our wide and wild families into the fold. It was so much fun. A few moments before we walked as newlyweds into the reception tent, our friend and caterer Becky found Robbie and said to him, "The wedding cake has been compromised," and he didn't know what that meant. But we later found out that the enormous cake and its wooden stand had been so heavy that the table underneath collapsed under its weight. Somehow enough of it was salvaged to cut and pass around. And recently I found a photograph of our reception in which our friend Donovan was on the dance floor, flat on his stomach. I told him I was so impressed he knew how to do the worm. But when I mentioned the worm, he said, "Tallu, I wasn't doing the worm, I slipped on someone's drink, and ended up face-down on the dance floor and couldn't move for a long ten minutes."

And then there was the attire of the wedding party. As we were preparing for our wedding, I found wide bolts of a gorgeous linen fabric with owls and cats that I wanted to use in the ceremony in some way. The fabric depicted a scene from a poem I was only semifamiliar with, but I loved everything about the design and feel of the fabric. After I had purchased dozens of yards of it, we had dinner with his parents, and I showed it to them. The four of us were trying to piece together the words of the poem, which we only kind of knew. So we looked it up, and I read it aloud at the table, with the first stanza going like this:

> *The owl and the pussycat went to sea*
> *In a beautiful pea-green boat,*
> *They took some honey, and plenty of money,*
> *Wrapped up in a five-pound note.*

That was about as far as we could collectively get with the words. But I kept on reading the rest of it from my phone out loud:

> *The owl looked up to the stars above,*
> *And sang to a small guitar,*
> *O lovely pussy! O pussy, my love,*
> *What a beautiful pussy you are,*
> *You are, you are!*
> *What a beautiful pussy you are!*

Oh my God. I was mortified speaking these lines aloud to my future in-laws at their kitchen table, in front of their eldest son.

Having just spent a small fortune on bolts of this fabric, which I could not, of course, return. Our entire wedding party wore handmade ties and dresses and skirts from this fabric despite the association with such a weird poem. And to this day, Robbie wears his linen bow tie every anniversary dinner, with both the owl and the pussycat in cheerful attendance alongside.

I love these memories, and reflecting on ten years of marriage has me thinking in new ways about the vows we make to another in marriage. We take vows, and we don't know even a fraction of what life is going to ask of us in our commitments. And it's not just that we don't know, it's that we can't know. When we pledge "in sickness and in health," we aren't generally considering the memory loss, the body slipping, the mind fading, or even the cancer that could show up in an otherwise healthy body at age forty. The possibility of any of these things seems so remote, as we button up our best clothes and select the flowers and consider the beef option or maybe the fish.

In my marriage, I have been noticed. I have been affirmed. Not always and not perfectly, but neither have I always given these things well. I have been challenged. I have been cared for. I have been celebrated. I have been called out, and I have been called in. I have shown my worst and been held through my struggle and self-doubt. I think Robbie and I can say, for all our loss and heartache that we face these days, that the gifts we have received in our marriage far outnumber our losses. Life, as I continue to experience in my marriage, will dash and devastate, all while handing you a damn dream come true.

Hair

After I passed the halfway mark of my radiation treatments during the round of chemo and radiation after surgery, my hair started falling out in handfuls. I still had enough hair in the right places to fashion a flap that covered up the large bald spot in the back left part of my head. The hair loss was a side effect of where the beam of radiation targeted, thus the hair loss on only one side. I know the majority of people receiving treatment for cancer lose their hair, and I am no exception. But I did have exceptional hair before! Iconic, thick, long blond hair.

When I was just starting out with Mobile Loaves and Fishes, a gaggle of hilarious sixth-grade boys volunteered every Wednesday afternoon. I think they were getting school credit for their community service, because the semester culminated in a report on the work they'd done each week. Addison, an open-hearted, hilarious boy, wrote his paper and turned it in to me to read. Instead of focusing on the work he accomplished with his peers or the complicated reality of food insecurity in our city, he spent three pages writing about his supervisor's—my—hair. How flowing it was, how blond. How long it was, and how I could tie it up in a knot without a hair tie.

Nearly twenty years ago, at the same church camp Bethany Hills, my friend Hope organized a powerful ritual concerning hair—one that I remember vividly. We were counseling high schoolers that summer, and the spring before, at a weekend retreat, she noticed all the long hair trailing down the backs of so many campers, and we hatched a plan. The plan was to invite campers—both girls and boys—to cut and donate their braided hair to an organization that provided haircuts free of charge and made wigs for children who needed them.

So during the camp in June, we participated in a worship service that began with a few people volunteering to get a single braid cut and placed on the altar. It was a time set apart, a ritual that honored gifts and generosity and left us all asking ourselves, *What do I have to offer in abundance?*

After the vespers service, we gathered on the lodge porch for the rest of the haircuts. Those with signed permission slips went first, and the act of giving was so palpable and moving that those first haircuts prompted dozens more. Campers without their parents' permission called home from the single landline in the director's cabin. A local hairstylist from a nearby small town had been retained to do the haircuts. Given the anticipated volume of braids and cuts, he emphasized to us several times that he wouldn't be able to do styles on anyone, just cut off the braids. We said great, but we could tell he was unsure about us and apprehensive about the whole plan.

This all went down on the night of the popular camp dance. Unbelievably, nearly no one was inside dancing, but instead we were all piled onto the porch, people holding each other's hands through the symbolic haircutting ritual. So many affirmations were offered, and our community was connected by a sense of generosity, joy, and love.

At the end of the long night, as a few of us were wrapping up, the stylist started to cry. He shared with us that as a gay man living in the South, he had never been invited into Christian spaces where he was accepted or supported as he was. But what a role he had to play and a gift he had to offer us that day. He helped to create this sacred moment, and in many ways he was the one shepherding us through this offering of what we had in abundance. The next morning Hope and the other counselors boxed up the braids, each safely tucked into its own gallon ziplock bag, and sent them on to the foundation that would transform each one into a blessing in someone else's life.

I realize now how many personal stories I have about hair, and how hair has been a meaningful point of connection and conversations about race, gender, sexuality, and other aspects of our intersecting identities. There was the time my friend Kym, a Black woman, didn't call me out but called me "in" to a conversation about the way some women of color perceived my near-incessant and then oblivious habit of playing with my hair in our grad school classroom. Or the time my friend Lauren, a white woman, shaved her head in college and so many in our community speculated and made assumptions about her relationships and sexual orientation. Hair! It is such a layered and complex part of human existence.

I think it's very human to feel two things at once. For example, I mourn the loss of my hair, and I know *it's just hair*. Even though it was beautiful by some standards, I do have enough perspective to know that it was never the source of my beauty. After the first few days of my radiation treatment, it came out in soft clumps. There was no resistance or tether to my scalp as there usually would be. It just quietly separated from my head and piled into my hand. The skin beneath it was so thin and tender.

So I placed the soft clumps of hair into the compost bin alongside whatever else was ready for discard and decomposition—coffee grounds, stems of greens, moldy berries, and all this hair—all of it, back into the earth from whence it came. I am practicing letting a part of myself go, a part I have loved. And maybe you are too.

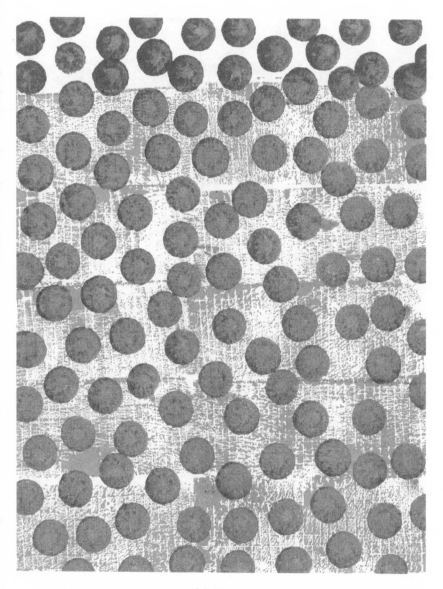

Into View

Rats

In 2019, before my cancer diagnosis, I was in the community-room kitchen at the Nashville Food Project, and a volunteer stealthily approached me to notify me, in a whisper, that when she pulled her pans of salad from the walk-in refrigerator for her truck run, she spotted a dead rat on the floor beneath the shelving. I walked back to the fridge with her to dispose of the rat. We got a broom and a dustpan, and yep, there was the bloated dead rat and its long tail beneath the shelf. As I watched it roll closer to the dustpan, I noticed how hard its body seemed, maybe from having been so cold in the fridge. As we made our final sweep into the dustpan, I started to laugh. Lo and behold, this was not a dead rat. It was a beet! A rat-shaped, raw, lone beet who'd lost its way. It went into the compost nonetheless.

My staff began posting pictures of the "dead" beet, and a local restaurant with a very robust community hour created a beer out of the story—Deadbeet Ale. I'm not a pied piper, but I think rodents, whether vegetables or not, have followed me my whole life.

My friend Lauren and I lived in an old cottage in the Tennessee woods when we were in college. The cabin was spacious and warm and home to so many mice. Our landlord asked us to set traps, so we bought them in packs of six and set them out during the winter months. In an evening, we could put out all six in the corners of our basement-level den, and within the hour all six would slap shut. Later, we'd descend the staircase together to confront the inevitable carnage. And we worked out a system to ease the pains of facing it. One of us used a pair of pliers to grab the mousetrap with the dead mouse; the person with this job got to wear a special pair of sunglasses, which we kept next to the pliers. The other one of us held out a doubled-up plastic bag, which we used to carry the dead mice into the woods to bury.

I've wanted to reach for some version of those sunglasses a thousand times. When I was in Nicaragua, at every single red stoplight, children and adults came up to my car's open window, begging me for money. It felt impossible to make eye contact with any one of them—whether to say yes, to say no, or even to say nothing. I'd rather have reached for some glasses and pretended to not see them, and all my guidebooks encouraged me to do some version of the very same thing.

It takes so much courage to see the world—a big claim that no small story can adequately accommodate. Especially when the world is right up in our face through an open window. But many of us have the opportunity to choose what to see and when. What a benefit it is to have choices! I know so much about living in big houses, living in big privileges, living into my very own big dreams. I live within easy reach of the glasses, the pliers, and the doubled-up bag, and I have a stack of guidebooks telling me exactly how to reach for them whenever I want them. And when they're not there to protect me from what the world really looks like, a hundred other freedoms are.

The Sugar on Top

Sunday worship in Nicaragua had a way of lasting hours upon hours. In many ways, these long-drawn-out mornings were lessons in patience and stillness, but they often became hours of just sitting. I recall one Sunday morning finally starting worship with our community and having communion. But the elements of the table consisted of small bananas and mango juice. There was no wine or bread, these were the things they had. But they were delicious, and I found out later that many communions there consisted of whatever extra sweet food they had nearby. I was used to communion with bland food, tart drink, and an air of seriousness, but the saccharine taste from those bananas gave me a new perspective. It was an unexpected part of a familiar ritual, but it was also a delightful sweet taste of local food.

Sometimes I have trouble embracing the sweetness in my life, however it unexpectedly and uncontrollably shows up. One spring we tapped the south-facing sugar maples in our front yard, and after boiling down ten-plus gallons of sap over two weeks, after making what seemed like fifty fires outside, eventually bringing the process inside so the steam could dirty our stove lights and attract bugs, we ended up with a half-pint of homegrown maple syrup. But man was it good, for a few meals at least. These were the same trees up the driveway from where Robbie and Lulah would wait for me occasionally when I would come home from a long day, a sweet surprise, with her one-year-old chubby legs bursting out of a onesie as he held her up for me to see her drooly smile.

When I was nine years old, I had the chance to fly to Pittsburgh all by myself to spend a week with my grandparents. It was summer, the height of berry season, and my grandparents took me to the country for a long weekend. Part of our fun was picking berries all day, and coming back to bake cobblers and pies. In my memory, my grandma and I baked and baked, but I can only remember a single family we actually delivered a cobbler to. It was my grandmother Tallu who truly painted with the big brush. And it would be just like her, and subsequently me, to make a dozen pies without thinking about who might be around to receive them.

Lulah, who's now nine herself, is strong-willed and capable in the kitchen too, and wildly creative. She makes grocery lists every week, wants a paid internship in the Nashville Food Project's kitchen, and begs me to help her "mis-en-place" for her kitchen projects. (This is an old French culinary technique to prepare ingredients ahead of time—I'm sure she gleaned the phrase from a show or a cookbook.) The scope of her big ideas overwhelms me, and now I know that's how my own mom must have felt as she figured out how to give me the space I needed to be me. Maybe she still does.

I obviously know that Lulah is not me and she is not mine, but when she gets an itch to bake a three-tier wedding cake for nobody in particular, it connects me to the mystery of my own life. I'm so grateful for that. And I try to stop—just like when her innocent face beamed at me in the long driveway of our old yard—to enjoy the sugar on top of it all.

Bones

Whatever is foreseen in joy
Must be lived out from day to day.
—WENDELL BERRY, *A Timbered Choir*

I had a therapist who once referred to the Nashville Food Project as my first child. Ha! How much of my best it has received. How much of my time, ideas, patience, devotion. When I first started running the day-to-day food program and managing volunteers, each week I followed a routine. I would load up my tiny car with snacks from Second Harvest Food Bank, shop for discounted sliced bread at Kroger, and sort through pallets of almost-expired yogurt. All for inclusion in the sack lunches that we delivered in our food trucks to people living on the streets or in camps, or staying in motels.

Then in the spring of 2010, we planted our first garden in the city. With no greenhouse or experienced farmer to speak of, we watered seeds in flats on the windowsills in my office. Like a miracle, those leggy plant starts became crates of fresh greens we shared with Cayce residents a couple of nights a week.

I remember the collards flew off the shelves of our truck, but the kale went untouched, despite being a very similar vegetable, prepared in very similar ways. Mention of this underlines the truth that every single one of our days doing this work taught me scores of lessons about people, communities, systemic issues, and best intentions, and how those of us trying to do good work so often miss the mark. However, this experience was just the beginning of realizing how much I *didn't* know. When the May 2010 flood hit Nashville, our volunteers were mobilized to help. We got a call asking if we could feed the Metro Water crews who were working twenty-four-seven to get the water line up and running after the flood had washed it out. In the three weeks that followed, our folks prepared and delivered more than nineteen thousand meals to those workers, as well as to thousands of Nashvillians in need. In many ways, it was these meals that showed us the way forward; we learned we could make nutritious meals from scratch for a crowd, and this relief effort introduced us to so many new friends who have been instrumental in our continued growth and evolution.

So with that experience in flood relief, a new vision called us for how our organization could respond to community needs, but it wouldn't happen overnight. We spent lots of time trying to figure out how to redefine our work, most of it at our first-floor headquarters in South Hall at Woodmont Christian Church, and in the basement room underneath.

I have spent so many hours in church basements in my lifetime. They are often semiworn spaces, furnished with secondhand chairs and couches, usually adorned with fake plants, random coffee cups, and extension cords—a fertile place for us to plant the seeds of our big ideas. The mismatched nature of these spaces is always in service of creating a comfortable place for people to gather, not unlike someone seeking out a twelve-step meeting or a recovery circle. This church space, imperfectly decorated by the leavings of so many who had come before us, reflected so perfectly our planning sessions.

With big ideas and a steady stream of extraordinary community support, we improved the quality of the meals we made, harvested more excellent produce in our gardens, increased the amount of food we recovered, and engaged more volunteers in the work of growing, cooking, and sharing.

And in the face of what every day felt like unlimited need, we shifted our focus from serving individuals to supporting communities with good food. In fact, one of the first things we asked new community partners was, How can good food support what's going on in your community? Once something becomes successful, it's easy to have revisionist history about how enjoyable the work has always been, but the work is and was made up of the hard things. The bones is the hard work of constructing a vision and piecing together the framework that keeps the vision running.

Over the years, our kitchens received such extraordinary food donations from generous kindhearted friends. We were connected to a relationship with a local organization, called Hunters for the Hungry, that provided ground venison each winter, supplying our kitchens with local lean deer meat for inclusion in our meals. Our friend Jimmy was always proud to donate a steer each winter. We received bags upon bags of overwintered organic spinach from a church congregation that planted a large vegetable garden for the express purpose of donating this food as nourishment for our community. And the kindest salt-of-the-earth couple Bill and Mary Ruth engaged the youth from their church in planting a large vegetable garden every year for their youth group to tend and harvest and donate the produce to our kitchens.

One of the more extraordinary gifts came in the form of a creative plan for the future. A generous friend envisioned a large and diverse apple orchard on the Cumberland Plateau, located about ninety miles from our headquarters in Nashville. In years, this land would bear local fruit, a treat like none other. Joe's vision required significant inputs as well as years of advance planning, to say nothing of a lot of human labor and financial resources. While he was investing in the orchard, he began bringing crates of apples in several local varieties, grown by other growers, to our kitchens so we could get the hang of receiving local fruit and making use of it in our programming.

In order to sufficiently resource our kitchens with food, we needed food donations of all sizes. I heard an illustration that really helped me envision our needs: If we are trying to fill up a jar with rocks, we will do our best to fill that jar up to the brim using both larger rocks and smaller rocks, even sand. It reminds me of receiving a telephone call one afternoon from an older woman. She told me she had a huge bumper cucumber crop that year, and could she bring over some cucumbers to our kitchen? Of course we would love it, we replied. Within the hour, she appeared at our kitchen door with a small paper sack of six cucumbers to be donated to the Nashville Food Project. How delightful!

There were so many innovative ways to resource our work. Generous school groups in our community held Empty Bowls events to foster awareness about local issues specifically related to food insecurity. One wonderful young man decided to do his mitzvah project in advance of his bar mitzvah, asking all who attended his service and celebration to bring a bottle of olive oil as a gift. He was then able to donate the olive oil to our kitchens in celebration of his coming of age. And finally a company that befriended us early on—they made metal airplane wings—so generously wanted to give back to our community that they configured and reconfigured lots of opportunities for their employees and executives to get involved. One day my friend Steve said that his company decided they'd go around the plant to pick up scrap metal, sell it, and donate the proceeds to us. I thanked him profusely, thinking we would get a couple thousand dollars, but when we received the first check, it was for more than $26,000. And those gifts came to us four or five more times!

Other food donations included outrageous amounts of meat, from national conference events located in Nashville, each event garnering hundreds and hundreds of pounds of fresh, never-before-frozen meat, all for inclusion in our made-from-scratch meals.

In the early years, we had plenty of space to cultivate the beginnings of what was functionally our baby start-up. But as the organization grew, our work expanded, our staff got bigger, our needs became more diverse, and we were running out of space constantly. At one point, three of my co-workers and I were all in the stage of breastfeeding our kids, and we took turns in the one semi-private space to pump breast milk. Meetings were held in the same room and at the same time as others, with maybe a makeshift barrier in between. But the bones were being constructed slowly, and the unsexy story of how we got our project and vision up and running was continuing, with big and small rocks filling up the jar each day.

Blessings Brightly Lit

We travelers, walking to the sun, can't see
Ahead, but looking back the very light
That blinded us shows us the way we came,
Along which blessings now appear, risen
As if from sightlessness to sight, and we,
By blessing brightly lit, keep going toward
That blesséd light that yet to us is dark.

—WENDELL BERRY, "Sabbaths 1999, VI"

I am moving through these days on the prayers of many. Lately I feel physically depleted, emotionally exhausted, and have cried so much and so hard. It feels like all my strength is required to do the daily things and make it to bedtime. My current list of medicines, including a strong chemo, is leaving in its wake a lineup of spectacular side effects: insomnia, weight gain, nausea, stomach pain, and for a little insult to injury, teenage acne. What a combo! A year and a half ago I remember strolling into Vanderbilt University's cancer center and feeling so vital and strong. But I am puffy now, and my vision is radically different, and when I look at myself in the mirror, I appear sick and changed. I guess that's because I am changed and changing, as I continue to adjust to living with this cancer.

My relative youth seems to be the primary thing going for me, something that my care team points back to often. I'm so grateful for that, and yet it is my young age that makes this diagnosis so shocking. I have known a few others who have lived with and died from glioblastoma, and most of them were elderly. But a friend from college, Anderson Bailey, died of glioblastoma at age thirty-seven after a one-and-a-half-year battle. He was a brilliant ceramic artist with a boundless creative and loving spirit. While we were in school, we taught a bunch of art classes together to children in rural Tennessee, east of Nashville, and he could capture the attention of an elementary school classroom like a birthday party magician. I've never met anyone else like him. A little while after his death, I walked into my local public library to vote. As I was waiting in line, I encountered a table set up with ceramic bowls made and donated by potters from all across the region. It was a project created in Anderson's memory and offered an opportunity for any library card holder to "check out" a handmade piece of pottery and feel it, use it, and enjoy it at home. Anderson's presence was so pleasurable, and I loved how this installation was geared toward not just utility but pleasure too—just like his gorgeous pots, many of which you can find in my kitchen cupboard today. Anderson was joy, and it was shocking to lose him so young and so quickly.

On a glioblastoma listserv, someone newly diagnosed asked a question of long-term survivors. A long-term survivor for this type of cancer is considered to be one who has been living with it for three or more years since diagnosis. "What's your secret?" the newly diagnosed listserv member asked. Answers ranged from taking specific supplements, to strictly adhering to a ketogenic diet, to petitioning God in prayer, to following extreme exercise regimens. One answer caught my eye: a member who offered, "I just live my life." What would it look like for me to just live my life? Living as I used to live before my diagnosis isn't the answer, and neither is living as though I don't have terminal cancer. Why do we live with the assumptions that the future we cannot yet see will give us both time and health?

But now I'm learning that facing death is teaching me how to live. Even in my sadness and exhaustion and longing, I feel an extra amount of gratitude for the regular stuff: my weekly work call with Christa and Teri, packing my kids' lunches, brushing their hair after showers at night, taking walks in the park across the street, eating dinner with our best neighbors, the Randolphs, and drinking coffee in the mornings with Robbie. All that: bliss! Recently I sat across the dining table from him at one of our favorite restaurants, Henrietta Red. We devoured an enormous platter of briny raw oysters with mignonette, and the warmth of the covered patio felt like a balm after all the ice and snow in Nashville. Looking at his gorgeous smiling eyes, I could not keep the tears back. My face mask became soaked, and I could not stop thinking about how good I've got it and how immense our mutual respect and love are for each other. It is so heartbreaking that we will not have all the years together that we want. He has been and remains so present and patient, and best of all, he is kind. Kindness. I think it is my favorite quality in a person. His kindness has made me kinder and taught me so much about being kind to myself and others. I feel so lucky to be the one on the receiving end of his loving gaze. Maybe "just living my life" is cherishing these regular times together, at our regular date night restaurant, eating our regular order, with this human I've been regularly loving for the last many, many years.

I have so many questions and fears, not just about human death in general terms but also about my death in particular. I have learned from my doctors that the brain can't feel pain, and yet it is the body center out of which pain is experienced. I have also learned that brain cancer is not metastatic, it does not travel to other parts of the body and do a fatal takeover of other organs. I've asked my oncologist what people with glioblastoma die from, or in other words, what I might die from. A brain hemorrhage? Cardiac event? Seizure? Coma? And will it be peaceful? I imagine I won't be alone when it happens, but will I feel alone? Will I be in our bed? Will Robbie sleep in that bed afterward? Will I be lucid and able to talk with my family? What will they witness at the event of my death? Will they be scared? Will I?

A few nights ago I was snuggling our son, Thomas, who is now seven years old. I was holding him and, unprompted, he started to pray, "Dear God, could you please make sure to take away all the cancer from my mom Tallu Quinn's brain? She's right here in the bed with me if you need to find her."

But the truth is that I have already been found. Even as I rage through this present sorrow to the unknowable future that will be my early death, I can look back into the past and see all who have loved and supported me. They are the *blessings brightly lit.* I encounter these blessings in the companionship of others—cards and texts and comments online, correspondence from people from decades past, even anonymous letters. And not to mention our minister friend Farrell's soup, our family's de facto godmother Muzzie's two-dollar bills in the mail for our children, generous and unexpected financial support, visitors from out of town, cozy blankets and quilts, and the memory of those pots gathered in Anderson's honor.

One weekend last year we were floored by a group of friends, mostly parents from the kids' school, who organized the

#TeamTallu 5K Walk/Run, a charity race in the middle of Covid that generated a sea of blue-shirted love and support from all over the country, including a blitz of happy photographs on social media. And together we raised nearly $60,000 for Vanderbilt-Ingram Cancer Center to fund medical research on this complicated and tenacious type of brain cancer! In all these myriad ways, friends are accompanying me as I walk into the blinding unknown of the future.

"The very light that blinded us shows us the way we came." I've been living with the profound poem by Wendell Berry for a decade, and its meaning is constantly being revealed to me. I love how it describes the future not only as dark, because we can't see into it yet, but also as a blinding light, since we encounter events ahead of us that we are confident will do us in or take us under. As we look toward them, they appear so difficult and insurmountable, yet we find faith and resilience and the company of many who journey with us. In all that, what appears to be impossible rises to some kind of embraceable blessing. We don't know that the difficulties of our present situation will reveal themselves as future blessings; we can't know. Getting terminal cancer at age forty was a blinding light, and yet in this last year, I have been found by Love and continue to be held in Love, while together we keep going toward this blessed light that is yet to us dark.

Watermark

As I approached my college graduation from art school, all final-year students were expected to create work that constituted a senior thesis, which would both showcase their technical ability and engage the viewer conceptually and aesthetically. A senior thesis show was typically a body of work in the student's field and focus. Because fiber arts encompasses such a wide array of mediums—from book arts to fabric design to weaving—I had to select one area to concentrate on and devote my creative energy and ideas to. My thesis work was titled "20 Plants, 20 Papers," and was a handsome, educational, and, I believe, unique exploration into both native Tennessee flora and the ancient art of hand papermaking.

One of the hand papermaking techniques I acquired in school is the tradition of a watermark. A watermark is typically noticeable only in handmade papers, and only when a dry sheet of paper is held up to a light source. It goes largely unseen unless one is looking for it. The watermark conveys a handmade quality and typically indicates what is special about the paper's weight and texture.

Professional artisans and traditional papermakers have used watermarks for millennia to add their own unique signatures on their craft—a mark of the maker. The best papermakers would create their own watermark by stitching their name or initials or small design into the mesh frame upon which the wet paper is made.

What I like about the watermark as a symbol is that it's not overt but a quiet signature, blended into the backdrop of the page—at once both unique and subtle. It's not a design applied on top of the page, which could be smeared away, but part of its very structure, embedded within it.

In trying to chart my own vocational path, I've often come back to these words of the poet David Whyte, who writes in *Consolations* about vocation:

> A true vocation calls us out beyond ourselves, breaks our heart in the process and then humbles, simplifies and enlightens us about the hidden, core nature of the work that enticed us in the first place. We find that all along, we had what we needed from the beginning, and that in the end we have returned to its essence, an essence we could not understand until we had undertaken the journey. . . . The authentic watermark running through the background of a life's work is an arrival at generosity. . . . Perhaps the greatest legacy we can leave from our work is . . . the passing on of a sense of sheer privilege, of having found a road, a way to follow, and then having been allowed to walk it.[1]

I love how light exists in relationship to the watermark: one needs the other for both discovery and then clarity. Holding the watermark up to the light source reveals its intricacy and illuminates the essence of its identity. At this point in my illness, I never will have a single professional identity, as I imagined I would in my younger years. But the many ways my life has invited me into meaningful work has left a mark in the background—quiet but indelible.

Whether I am making paper, growing food, cooking meals, loving people, or starting a family, I feel I am my most authentic self, noticing my watermark, when I am doing or creating with my hands, heart, and mind. All my life many have held up the light for me, a part of the sheer privilege I have experienced along this path and a reminder of my own responsibility to shine it back for others. Those light bearers manifest the divine, and the light continues to leave its mark on the days I have left, before the final sheet is drawn and the last wet page is set.

One poem that has accompanied me through my theological journey and my vocational life is the following piece from a phenomenal Kentucky poetess named George Ella Lyon. Ever since I happened upon it in a stunning anthology of poetry called *Cries of the Spirit* that I bought in Nashville from the great Davis-Kidd Booksellers in 2002, the marked-up and dog-eared pages of her poem have been a part of how I approach difficult questions when I have become paralyzed or galvanized by the world. I am honored, after getting to ask George Ella personally for her permission, to include it here.

INVENTING SIN
GEORGE ELLA LYON

God sings to us
        We cannot read
She shouts
        We take cover
She shrugs
        and trains leave
        the tracks

Our schedules! we moan
Our loved ones!

God is fed up

All the oceans She gave us
All the acres of steep seedful forests
And we did what
        Invented the Great Chain of Being
        and the chain saw
        Invented sin

God sees us now
        gorging ourselves and
        starving our neighbors
        starving ourselves and
        storing our grain
and She says

    I've had it

You cast your trash
upon the waters
It's rolling in

You stuck your fine finger
into the mystery of life
to find death
and you did

Learned how to end the world
in nothing flat

Now you come crying
to your mommy
    Send us a miracle
    Prove that you exist
Look at your hand, I say
Listen to your sacred heart
Do you have to haul the tide in
sweeten the berries on the vine

I set you down
a miracle among miracles
You want more—
It's your turn
You show me

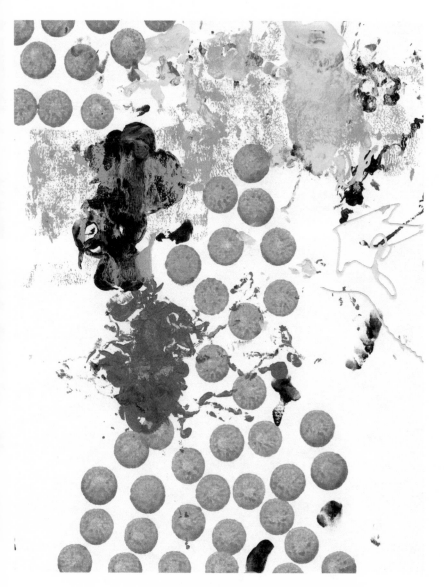

Collisions

Ordinary Rituals

I love to hear my friend David, and many other staff and volunteers I've worked with over the years, tell me stories about the outrageous, unglamorous tasks they've had to take on in the name of food justice. They've picked up day-old bread that was left for recovery by major grocery chains, fruit arrangements the day after a local gala, and cases of quinces. (One has to ask oneself in some of these scenarios, Was this case of quince worth it? What does one even do with quince?) They tell of bringing buckets of tools to a garden site on a daily basis, unloading a dozen heavy bags of diatomaceous earth, making multiple trips to a compost facility in Franklin, even taking a hurt chicken from a community garden to a volunteer's house so her surgeon-husband could stitch it up.

My experience is that this work has always been heavy and unglamorous, but it has been joyful. Working with one's hands, like most physical activity, has a wonderful way of flossing out the mind. Hauling this stuff to and from for the last decade and making something meaningful has been messy and strenuous and yet somehow joyous. Our slogan internally evolved to become "come be part of our joy." And anyone who's hung out at the Nashville Food Project for any amount of time knows that there is a constant, vibrant chaos that's in passionate, hopeful pursuit of what we think is possible for Nashville, and what we believe Nashvillians are capable of doing together to wail against the symptoms of poverty. Wendell Berry says "good work is a source of pleasure," and that is what comes to my mind when I remember these stories.

And this joyful chaos also had many regular patterns built into it. Large groups of people practiced lots of little rituals: unloading a truck of rescued food from Whole Foods on Monday mornings, setting up the tables for meal prep every day, taking weekly farm walks at the refugee-led Growing Together farm to determine what's ready for market, awarding a khaki apron to a kitchen volunteer after six months of regular commitment, laying out the tablecloth for meal service for veterans at Operation Stand Down Tennessee each Wednesday at noon, planting the garlic every October and harvesting it the following June, turning the compost piles every chance we got, and the list went on and on. Rumi wrote, "Let the beauty we love be what we do. / There are hundreds of ways to kneel and kiss the ground."[1]

These rituals bound our weeks and months and years. These rituals are containers, offering us a rhythm and routine in which we ask ourselves and each other the hard questions: Why is there so much waste in our food system? In this land of plenty, why don't people have enough food to eat? What is the significance of growing vegetables from small seeds? What is the meaning of feeding other people?

A ritual invites us to practice what we wish were true, but may not be true yet. Growing, cooking, and sharing good food are all activities that offer us the chance to practice generosity, hospitality, creativity, justice, patience, and love. The world is full of suffering, injustice, and deepening divides. And yet as one of God's ongoing gifts of Creation, food is constantly renewing and restoring. And while the work is not explicitly faith-based, all of it is sacred. There is an inherent joy and fundamental blessing to be found in good food, especially when it includes the most marginalized among us. Our team understands these activities as our sacred calling and our primary responsibility, even though we didn't invent the script for these things. Ours is a place of healing, where these ritual acts are practiced and taken seriously for how they can change our hearts and our lives. For what we practice plays a significant role in how we live our lives.

A while back I heard the Jesuit priest Father Greg Boyle of Homeboy Industries in Los Angeles speak about the Christian sacrament of communion. He said something about how "Jesus is concerned we'll forget not that the cup is sacred but that it's ordinary." Somewhere along the way in my theological formation, I think I was taught that spiritual life is something still, something stopped in time, something carved away from the ordinary world or rhythm of a regular day. But as I get older, I see examples of prayer all around me that look more like chores. They are varied and endless and they are ordinary: cooking a meal, setting a table, planting trees, taking someone's temperature, turning compost, feeding animals, packing a child's lunch, weeding garden beds, mowing the lawn, raising children. All these, when practiced mindfully, can clear the head, open the heart, reconnect us to something hopeful, and create space in the day to praise the living world.

A New Knot

In Nicaragua I passed a long weekend sitting in a rocking chair that didn't rock anymore because one of its bowed legs was snapped off in the back. It seemed like everything there was broken or almost broken or was at one time broken and was half-repaired with a belt or an old bra strap. A few nights before, I went home from my office and found Martha, the Nicaraguan woman I lived with, fixing the nasty, gnawed-up clicker for the TV with some Super Glue and a crayon. She was listening to "Crocodile Rock" when I walked in! Elton John's *Greatest Hits* was the only CD they had that didn't skip, and I think we listened to it eighteen or nineteen times that Saturday afternoon.

Passing a day there was like taking a lesson in knotting—how to make double knots out of bungee cords and pieces of old rubber hose, figuring out how to tie one outrageous situation to the next one, and how to make all the ends meet. Things that are usually so simple were so complicated, and regular daily life was held together by whatever old things would reach. When I walked into my room and turned on my overhead light, it only sometimes worked. It was suspected that a neighbor was stealing electricity from our wires—a totally hilarious claim since our electricity was already spliced half a dozen ways to feed power to our cluster of homes. When I went into my bathroom to wash my hands in the sink, the faucet only sometimes worked, because there was a leak in our pipe, so we kept the main line turned off. When we needed water, we walked down the street to unscrew it—not a huge deal except when it was the middle of the night and I had no clothes on and my bedroom door was stuck in its frame if it was a humid night, which seemed like every night.

My taxi driver Gregorio was late in the mornings, and when we weren't running out of gas, which was almost once a day, a tire was flat, or we drove in the night without headlights or the clutch just fell off onto the car floor. People showed up late to places, and they might call to say they were coming, or not coming, but chances were good one of our cell phones was out of minutes, so the call wouldn't go through. Passwords to semireliable wireless connections got changed, and no one knew the new ones or who we might ask to find out or why the old one stopped working in the first place. There was no haste in solving any of these problems or getting answers to any of these questions, and I assumed the chain of command for finding out was probably broken anyway.

But something held daily life together—maybe it was God or the strength of human will, or maybe it's just that daily life has to keep going, because what would be the alternative? I sat in Gregorio's piece-of-shit car and resented him for continuing to drive it. And I turned on the dry faucet or woke up to turn off the overhead light when it came on three hours too late. Or sang along to Elton John again and then again, and again. And those were the times I had to pull from some small spool of patience and faith and gratitude to tie a knot and try to hang on.

That weekend in the rocking chair I had been there for twenty-three days, and I was counting the days before I planned to leave. I figured out the numbers when I was talking to my friend Julia on the phone; it was so good to hear her voice over the line until the call was dropped, without warning. I walked down a few houses to the shop where I usually refilled my phone minutes, but that night they were only selling minutes for the other cell phone company. I had all the Spanish words to ask why, but not enough to collect a good answer, if there even was one. So I walked home to the rocking chair that did not rock, and I just sat still there and thought about how making it through one day is tethered to having made it through the day before. It was a simple cord that was holding all that together, maybe as thin as the thinnest thread. And surely the broken heart, the broken Spanish, the broken pipe, and the breaking-down car were testing the strength of it. But learning how to tie a new knot with paper clips and extension cords is learning the lesson about hanging on—which is what I did that night, which is what I'm still doing now, and it's what I'll wake up and do again tomorrow.

Chickenman

Right after our wedding, Robbie and I inherited six laying hens from a pastor friend of ours who had been called to another church and was moving out of the state. This same pastor friend also happened to be the one who taught a class we took on keeping backyard chickens. As my father-in-law was quick to point out, we literally inherited our teacher's pets.

A few days before we picked up our chickens, we secured our backyard from predators. We walked the privacy fence, looked for any holes under the house, and leveled a steep hill to detract hungry animals from climbing over. We found the shadiest spot for the position of the coop, bought pine shavings, wheat straw, organic feed, and a waterer. We purchased a coop from an older couple west of town and asked our neighbors for help unloading and assembling it. We set out fresh bedding for the chickens, and then came the babes—all different colors, all different breeds. We gave each one a name: Marin (named for Marin County, California, where we spent much of our honeymoon), Fanny Lou (after Fanny Lou Hamer), Nina Simone, Nopalita, Lady Bird (named for our friend and church member), and Toby Ziegler (for our favorite *West Wing* character). We became attached in an instant, learned their personalities, invited our parents over to meet the grandchicks, practiced picking them up, ate their delicious eggs, and doted on them in public, showing people pictures of them on our phones.

Their second night with us, I had to be downtown for work until late. After a while, I noticed I'd missed four calls from Robbie. Then came the text: "I lost some chickens." I called back to get more information. My husband was panicked: it was dark, and he could find only two of our little brood of six. He'd checked the coop numerous times, under the house, under the porch, behind the shed, inside the shed, the coop again. He hadn't heard any sounds of struggle—which would have been an indication that an opossum or raccoon had gotten inside the fence. Before we hung up, he said his plan was to hit the pavement and take a flashlight into the neighborhood to see if he could find any sign of our chickens, dead or alive.

I got home an hour later and walked into a sad, quiet house. Robbie was lying in a dark bedroom with a pillow over his face. He hadn't had any luck finding the chicks in the neighborhood. We discussed all the possible ways and reasons our chickens were gone: a predator had found its way in and made off with four of our girls; their wings weren't clipped as well as we'd thought and they'd flown over the tall fence; there was some sort of hole or exit beneath our house that was accessible to them but invisible to us. After all this positing, we concluded that we just weren't ready to be chicken parents, and we went to bed sad.

The next morning at six A.M., Robbie got up to let our two remaining chickens out of the coop, and all six of them marched right out of their little door. He came back up to our bedroom with a huge grin on his face and a look of confusion. All of them had been inside the coop all along, we discovered, just up on their roosting poles. Every time my sweet husband had lifted the lid of the coop to see if they were inside, they were roosting up on the top portion, the part of the coop in his hands. We were so excited to see them that morning that we had a little party out back, in our pj's, with breakfast and coffee. We are still laughing at what those chickens must have been thinking each time they were tipped sideways in the dark that night. It would make a great cartoon.

We all spend so much time looking for what's right before us, in front of us, inside us. We search for God, for ways to be faithful, for something to deliver us from present worry or strife. It's not wasted time, but when we catch a glimpse of God living right where we live, we remember our deliverance has already been sent.

Drinking the Poison

When I was in high school—I can't recall which year—I was given the citizenship award on the last day of school. I remember being so surprised to be getting an award, and I also remember coming home to look up the word *citizenship* in the dictionary to understand what it meant and whether I really had it.

I haven't felt like a very engaged citizen lately, but I am grateful so many people I love are. Yet I'm aware enough to know that these are difficult days for our nation. When Covid-19 spread across the United States, it disproportionately affected people of color. The political climate is more divided than I have ever known it to be in my lifetime. The movement for Black lives calls for a crucial racial reckoning for justice after centuries of white supremacy and institutional violence. The earth is groaning from the abuse of unchecked human consumption and "business as usual." The economic disparities shaped by policies that favor a few while so many fight over the crumbs left behind have resulted in a scarcity mindset in a true land of plenty. The diseases of despair that so many struggle with daily have a way of overshadowing whatever hope and resilience we might typically cling to.

Add to this the personal battles each one of us may be waging—cancer, addiction, infertility, unemployment—and it's a wonder anyone gets out of bed anymore.

My mom called me recently to jokingly let me know she was thinking about divorcing my dad. I laughed and asked what was going on, and she said she had a suspicion about how my dad voted. My dad—not a fan of either presidential candidate in the 2020 election—made a planned trip to Nashville the following day. When he arrived in our home, I broached the subject of the presidential election with him. Even considering the possibility that he could vote for someone who to me seems so hostile felt personally offensive. How could someone I respect so much possibly cast a vote for someone whose politics, behavior, belittling demeanor, decisions, and very presence I find so egregious? After talking for a while, my dad said, "Can we stop talking about this? I love you too much."

Sometimes I feel like I was born at the wrong time. The vitriol and division, the sophisticated killing machines, the corporations that have more rights than many humans do, the myriad ways we poison our planet, the gross inequity, the constant looking at screens, the lives of disposable convenience. I know these things existed in their own expressions in previous decades, but in times of despair for humanity, I find myself doing some revisionist history and waxing poetic about bygone days. But the truth is that there has been progress, and I enjoy the access and rights afforded to me as a result of that progress.

Anyway, I don't actually know who my dad voted for, or whether he voted for president at all. As a citizen, that's his right alone to know. But that night after a good twenty-four hours of knotting myself up with anger about it, I built a big fire in our front yard. I made a huge salad and brought it out to the fire. Neither of my kids wanted to eat the salad, and both had a hunger-induced meltdown. Robbie took them inside, and I sat my angry ass down on a stump and ate four bowls of the salad and stared into the fire alone. I thought about the election and all it symbolized in that moment, and I also thought about my dad, who's taught me so much about honesty, respect, generosity, and even citizenship. Eventually he joined me around the fire, and when it was time to go in, we untangled the long water hose and put out the flames.

I heard an expression once—that staying angry at another person is like drinking the poison and expecting the other person to die. There is righteous anger, and it's our duty as citizens to stay awake to the grievances of humanity. I don't want to lose sight of that, but before going to sleep that night, I decided I'm not going to fight with my dad about politics anymore. The days are too precious, and I love him too much.

Our Thin Veneer

Our kids, like many I'm sure, are so sensitive, especially about animals. One year on vacation, my mom took them to a dingy beach shop to get their own pet hermit crabs. Lulah's crab escaped or was snatched by something outside overnight, but we made it back home with Thomas's crab, which he named Teddy. And he and Robbie decided to get watering sponges, rocks, sand, moss, crab food, a chalk supplement, and even extra shells for this crab. At the time, we were so busy, and I didn't want to add any more daily responsibilities. But of course when Lulah went to the same shop a year later, she brought back Ginger Snap the crab to join Teddy.

Then a friend told us, a few months into having two crabs, that these kinds of crabs can live for up to twenty years! But what were we going to do but take care of the crabs? And the inchworms we found. And the baby robins we found in the yard that had fallen from a tall magnolia tree. They didn't survive longer than a few days, but the kids named them Hint and Mint and still talk about them.

Years ago visiting some friends in New York, I told them that I thought it was the most magical thing that we could put an ear into a big seashell's opening and hear the ocean. They laughed, looked at each other, and told me it was not the sound of the ocean inside the shell but the sound of my own blood pumping through my veins. It took several minutes before I believed them, and that was only after sitting on their couch, putting my ear into an empty coffee mug, and hearing, of all things, the ocean.

One morning a few years later, while walking at the beach on Jekyll Island in Georgia, I found a small door on the beach—thin and translucent—the kind that serves to wall up a conch inside its shell. In its glassy surface, I could see evidence that the shell door grew as the animal living behind it grew. It's amazing that a big, wet muscle of an animal can live with only a delicate veneer of protection from the salty, rocking world around it.

Some of us still believe that an empty shell has a pumping heart inside it that sounds like the ocean, and we wear skin that's thin for believing in old natural magic—skin that's etched with the residue that feeling deeply leaves all across our outsides. I once wore a capital letter *S* out to a bar in Manhattan during grad school—scribbled on a scrap of paper and taped to my chest. An *S* for sensitive, as in *Please be gentle with me tonight, I'm feeling very sensitive.*

We are permeable, penetrable, and wide open to believing in the saltiest stuff of the world. And when it hurts to live like that, we wonder if we've shown ourselves too much or let too much past our thin veneer of a door. I once asked a church youth group why they cared so much about organizing their Youth Sunday worship service, to work as hard as they were working. One of them said, "It's just the way our hearts are." Yes.

When I put my ear to the opening of where I come from, I can hear my mom and dad, and they sound like the widest ocean—

still in a love with each other that has been watered by their commitment to stay open, honest, vulnerable, and together. And with my ear to all this, I realize I'm listening to my own life too. It's no wonder my brothers and I feel so deeply and wear this tender skin, because we were born in their tide, and belong to it, and have tossed around in it our whole lives. And the same now with my kids.

I found that thin, glassy oval on the beach because at some point the conch shed that door and slugged its way into another shell, where it grew a thicker door. Even for the ways I wish I could shed some of my sensitivity or grow a thicker door, I don't really want to be anyone else. And I'm glad the sound of my blood pumping through my veins sounds just like the ocean. I think I'll keep listening for it, because that's just the way my heart is.

Table in the Wilderness

My luminous grandmother Tallu and her equally luminous younger sister, my aunt Betty, taught me and my cousin Sarah Wylie a little ditty when we were children. They said, "Repeat after us, 'Mable, Mable, get off the table, the two dollars is for the beer.'" And repeat we did! In our singsong young voices, we said it over and over and taught it to our younger siblings and a gaggle of younger cousins. I was probably thirty when I stopped to consider what the words actually meant.

But in fact, this chapter of my life finds me spending loads of time each week up on different tables. There was the radiation table—where the kind radiation therapists snapped me into place. As I lay down on the table, the machine delivered radiation to a very small hole that allowed for precision in the area of my tumor. There is the portable massage table of the incredible James, my friend and licensed massage therapist and healer to many, who visits weekly, double-masked and toting his speaker and playlist of comforting music for our sessions. And there is the table of my friend Rita, an energy worker and healer who invites me, as I lie on her heated table, to go on a journey centering the strength of God's spirit within. In these sessions, I find a place of sacred healing with my breath, with my hopes, and with surrender.

In all these different sessions, I often tear up or bawl. It can be so vulnerable to lie prostrate, faceup, without protection, in the company of another. Time spent on these tables feels slowed down, without movement, without the convenient distractions I often turn to. Despite the heavy emotions, I have so much gratitude for the privilege of engaging in these modes of healing and treating the cancer and the many physical, emotional, and spiritual side effects of the treatment.

I heard the Buddhist teacher Tara Brach say, in a dharma talk online, that "the joy is in getting real." We long for what is meaningful and what is real. In my searching, I am trying to distill all the noise into what is most basic, what will nourish me as I continue down this path that I do not want to be on at all.

My favorite tables are not set fancy but are sturdy and simple. Give me a drink in a jelly jar and crusty bread and good butter. If there's a bit more room and forethought, let's add bitter fresh greens with nothing but an uncomplicated vinaigrette and some salty cured meat. Seated around the table, give me real people who are ready to have real conversations and set aside all the pomp and circumstance of what is false, hollow, hateful, worldly, or avaricious. At the table, talk with me about your regrets, your peculiarities, your memories of your ancestors even if painful, the magic you have encountered, your great love, your fear, your shame, or your hope for the world.

Engaging in these practices connects me to my hopes for the future. In my mind's eye, the path ends at a sturdy stone table in the wilderness, and what happens there is real and forever. There is no pain there, no hate, no walls, no shame. The people gather and bring their best because that is all they carry there, and all they have, and it is offered freely, wholly, and it is real.

Flutters

Only Half Alone

When I woke
I was alone
—MARY OLIVER, excerpt from
"Five A.M. in the Pinewoods"

During my time working in Nicaragua, I spent so many hours there feeling lonesome. There was the problem of language—my Spanish was poor; and the problem of money—I had so little that I had to ration it in order to make phone calls. One late evening I was using my last purchased minutes to talk with my friend David, who was back home in New York. I was probably complaining about something. While we were talking, a wet dead rat fell out of my cardboard ceiling and landed at the foot of my bed with a splat. It was the same bed I was sitting in. "David! Some kind of dead rodent just fell out of the ceiling and landed on my bed." He was even more hysterical than I and suggested we get to work airlifting me out of there immediately. Feeling as lonesome as I did then, I can still remember how good it felt to laugh with him on the phone. I faced the large dead rat only half alone.

In Nicaragua the people I worked alongside and learned from

were exceptional—brilliant, bright, faithful, and incredibly patient with me. Yet in nearly every interaction I had there, I felt a little bit alone. This was no one's fault, only the normal feeling any stranger in a strange land has in a situation like the one I was in. I always had the sense that I couldn't fully show them who I was, and in turn, I couldn't ever fully know them for all they were. I was simultaneously surrounded by people I deeply respected and wanted to know, and exhausted at the end of every day from all the effort of trying. In some very raw and human way, even as lonesome as I was, the best part of every day was making it back into my own room and shutting my bedroom door for a long night, finally alone.

God was my closest companion during that time. There was no language barrier with God, no getting frustratingly lost in translation. And there was no smartphone or texting or streaming to hide behind. I cried every day. I prayed constantly. I wrote to God while also feeling like God was writing the story too. It's funny how we can, in hindsight, look back on an incredibly difficult time and remember it with fondness. When I lived there, all I wanted was to go home, and here I am typing away about how close I felt to God and how that time was a true crucible for learning to love myself and coming to know myself as unconditionally loved.

I have experienced intense times of loneliness in my life. The lump in my throat when my parents dropped me off at college comes to mind. The disorienting loneliness I experienced traveling and living abroad. And that painful distance I have felt in some of my closest relationships, even in my own strong marriage. And despite the near-constant presence of those I love completely, I have felt so lonesome in this illness too.

But I have never felt all the way alone. In my earliest memories, I've had an always-present sense of God within me, close to me, hitched to me the way my breath is. This benevolent presence is not something I earned or was owed or applied for or remember receiving at some discrete moment in time. God's loving presence has just been a truth of my life, and it's been in the emptier, slowed-down, or even painful times that I can feel this divine love and the strength of her company the most.

In seminary, there was always this theological question that we students would pivot back to again and again: Does prayer influence outcomes, or does prayer (simply or not so simply) change the one who is praying? Both? I hope prayer has the power to influence outcomes, and I know prayer has changed me. Softened my rough edges, slowed down my anger, increased my capacity to hope, provided courage, and many other things I'm not even aware of.

My understanding of what prayer is has changed in my adult years. I used to polish the prayers I would offer publicly when I worked in churches. There's nothing wrong with that, but it's not really my jam anymore. My dad was a songwriter in Nashville for a long time, and he wrote a song called "The Prayer of a Desperate Man." It was never listed on the *Billboard* charts, but people tell me often, at the grocery store or at the airport, that that song changed them. One of the lyrics is "He's known me from my birth, / and I think he roams the earth / for the prayer of a desperate man, / 'cause that's what he understands."

This is an exhausting, emotional illness. I am experiencing life at half-mast a lot of the time. Like attempting to communicate in a language I don't really speak, trying to translate to others how I see and what I feel can be lonely. My prayers these days are pretty desperate, completely unpolished, and so immense they aren't even offered in words, just tears.

But what pulls me out of my fear and loneliness are prayers of thanksgiving—naming what I am grateful for—habitually, outrageously, daily. With these prayers, I breathe in and out, and draw nearer to the Love who created me, surrounds me, resides within me. And it is the same Love who will carry me into that great beyond, I believe and I pray.

Living with a Body

I am poured out like water,
*   and all my bones are out of joint;*
my heart is like wax;
*   it is melted within my breast;*
my strength is dried up like a potsherd,
*   and my tongue sticks to my jaws;*
you lay me in the dust of death.

      —PSALM 22:14–15

In my midtwenties, on a trip to Denver with my friends John, Juls, and Andy, we went out and danced late into the night. The next day we rehashed the evening and how much fun we had dancing, and John said to us, "It's just so fun to have a body." I remember feeling that way, too.

But with this cancer, the daily retinue of pills, and the bimonthly chemotherapies, living in my body feels burdensome. My nasal passages are so dry they bleed. The smallest bump against the wall or car door turns into a massive purple-green bruise that lasts for weeks. My teeth are unbelievably sensitive to hot and cold. I eat constantly, and my knees groan under the weight gain I have experienced from the steady stream of steroids I take. My skin is itchy, and my nail beds are cracked and bleeding. I crave crunchy foods, but my cheeks are so big that when I chew, I accidentally bite down on the interior of my enormous jowls and catch the inside of my mouth, and the bleeding doesn't stop, but I can't seem to stop eating either. All this physical pain is new to me.

Most of these body changes are a result of the medicines I take, not the cancer itself. Anyone who has been on a regimen of steroids knows that the benefits come with significant side effects that can really change the shape of their body. The high dosage of steroids in my daily lineup has altered the eating and sleeping habits I've been accustomed to. The weight gain has been bringing me down and making me feel so uncomfortable. Thank goodness everyone else has also been wearing sweatpants during the pandemic! My puffy, moon-shaped face looks like someone I hardly recognize in the mirror, and my clothes don't fit. But the steroids keep the swelling down in my brain, and reduced swelling means fewer seizures, so I take these medicines that are imperfect but supportive nonetheless, and learn to live with the bloating and the unusual food cravings and the distended stomach and the gas and the sleepless nights.

There is such a deep loneliness in being really sick. The companionship of the divine is profound. But the late nights alone, the foggy confusion, the constant flow of people in and out—it is isolating. The great irony about the loneliness is that my mailbox is full every afternoon, the generous voicemails I receive go unreturned, I rarely pick up the phone anymore, and it's not like people aren't actively, patiently, generously reaching out. They are, and at a volume I can't even really grasp or respond to. And most of it is words and talk, something I need so much from my nearest and dearest, but something that I can only digest at certain times and in what feels like smaller and smaller amounts.

Friends have been asking me how the conversations with my children are going and how we talk about my illness and imminent death. And I have some answers, although I honestly feel most connected in love about our sad reality when I can just hold them and not have a long conversation. Something about the physical feel of Lulah and Thomas in my lap, or their hands in mine, feels the most connecting and thus healing, much more than words can join us or explain this. What words could possibly offer enough spaciousness to contain both the love and the sorrow that will allow us to heal? It feels like tending to our physical link is the balm that helps us enter into the pain of this and also somehow release it.

I've had the privilege of doing a lot of talk therapy over the last twenty years—sitting on the proverbial couches of brilliant psychotherapists, as well as participating in group therapy and recovery circles in different settings. This work has been such a crucial part of my adult life and spiritual healing and understanding of myself as a person, parent, partner, boss, and more.

But words can't heal everything. Since my cancer diagnosis, I have found so much healing in massage—spending my money and time on modalities of healing that are more physical, with the body at the center. Maybe it is because I am too talked out and exhausted for traditional talk therapy, or maybe it is because my body is so vulnerable in this illness. But every week I am grateful for the physical gifts of massage I receive from James, who begins his visits by setting up his strong table in our home and locating the strings holding me together. Finding each ligament, he gets them back into alignment with the masterful skill of which he is a most trustworthy and professional practitioner. At my request, he even massages the gas out of my belly. I know! The gifts of these human hands! And the human will for healing.

In college, my friend Lauren and I enrolled in a community course in beginning reflexology, and we've been exchanging foot rubs ever since. That is more than twenty years of propping up pillows between us with towels and lotions and massaging each other's feet—through pregnancies and big personal decisions and now cancer. Since I have been sick, it's been Lauren who has blessedly been doing the foot-rubbing, with me drifting off to sleep or crying into the pillows. Our time together may be my favorite and most healing gift these days. I see now how "doing feet," as we have called it, has been a treasured ritual within our friendship. We don't have to have any words and can experience the joy and the sorrow of the world through our bodies and the physical, healing presence that moves between us.

I am sensitive to how I write about the body, since I know so many people have experienced significant trauma that they continue to carry physically—abuse and assault in many forms. What a beast it is to have a body—a receptacle of shame, a center of pain, a container of malignancy. And what a joy too—exuberant joy, primal joy, expressive joy. I want to claim my body as a center of healing. I don't want to do any more harm but heal what I can, which is probably not much. There are pieces of my past and myself that I can pull gently closer, locate where the hurt lives, consider how that hurt has hurt others, find its tension, and do my best to release it.

I could write a long-ass chapter about the many food-related healing interests I have tried on for size. There was the short-lived juice "cleanse" my friend David and I attempted in New York. We packed up a hundred pounds of fresh produce—fresh horse-radish root, I recall—to juice and drink and thereby "remove toxins" from our bodies—which isn't even scientifically possible, I now understand. We piled these vegetables into bags and schlepped them from Manhattan to Fishers Island on a ferry, where we drank juice for approximately six hours and then decided to quit because we were ravenous and the juiced horseradish was so wretched.

I had another fascinating "master cleanse" moment when a college housemate introduced me to a fourteen-day cleanse consisting of nothing but organic lemon juice, grade B maple syrup, cayenne pepper, and filtered water. This liquid diet will clean out a person all right! I mean, what else could it possibly do? And then there was the time my mother-in-law Kay and I decided to try a gallbladder cleanse we'd read about in a magazine. The process consisted of chugging a very large amount of extra-virgin olive oil mixed with some organic lemon juice, after eating raw salads for three days. The olive oil and lemon mixture went down so thick and was so incredibly unpleasant to ingest. We gag when we recall the memory of chugging what was functionally a huge jar of salad dressing, sitting on the hood of her Cadillac sedan in a parking lot. Oh the laughing, healing tears come just from remembering these stories with fondness.

But I would be remiss if I didn't talk about how much food really has healed me and continues to heal me. Currently, I have found myself in a nightly obsession with making broths. First I tried shiitake mushrooms and parsley stems and the dried-out thyme from the crisper drawer of the fridge. Then I moved on to a nice piece of oxtail with a little apple cider vinegar and plenty of carrots and celery and onion. Lately I've been appreciating the benefits of whole packs of chicken wings and chicken feet for the gelatin they ooze and offer to the hot pot, paired with a lot of chopped fresh ginger. I drink this stuff three times a day with fermented vegetables, and if this sounds at all irritating, I completely understand. I am beside myself with curiosity over this middle-of-the-night fascination. So much of this gelatinous stuff is coming out of our kitchen now that no one leaves my house without a quart. The broths calm my raging stomach like nothing else. I think the hot liquid is the antidote to all the crunchy foods and my bulging gut, and it feels so good on my parched throat.

I guess today I am just all talked out, but my body aches for its own conversation. It has its own whole language. I am sicker than I have ever been and am still faithfully, scrappily striving to heal. My lips hurt. My throat is dry. My skin is cracked. Come drink this broth with me, and we can get quiet. I can't walk the neighborhood fast like I used to, but my aching feet cry out for touch. I can't find the words to reflect how confused I feel in my fuzzy brain, but will you rub the tender scar stretched across the back of my skull? I can't find any more words to explain the limits of my eyesight, but I can close my eyes into a folded prayer made of one breath in and one breath out.

Someone Up Close

Late in Tennessee summers, in my own garden and in the gardens that the Food Project maintains for food production and community use, the tall tomato plants are heavy with big green, yellow, orange, and red tomatoes—grape-shaped, round, or tiny cherry-sized. You can pick them early and fry them, or pull the cherry ones ripe, right off the vine, and unavoidably pop them into your mouth like candy. My mom and I usually buy boxes of "seconds" from the farmers market and spend one day in August canning them. And they'll eventually be used in pasta sauce or salsa. I'm not particular to tomato pie or BLTs, but I've known many a convert to those dishes in this country.

In 2013 a new program got off the ground in our community gardens called Growing Together, where refugees mainly from Bhutan and Burma planted seeds, tended plants, and then sold the results from dedicated garden plots. They grew unlikely crops, many of them native to their homes, and the program now has a vibrant CSA that supports the farmers. When we asked them what they would do with late-summer tomatoes if they had to prepare a featured dish for the Nashville Farmers Market, they suggested *achaar*, a tomato-based chutney popular in Bhutanese and Nepalese cuisine that can be made in combination with cilantro, mint, and peppers. Served alongside lentils and basmati rice, it's a fantastic, flavorful addition.

In these years since Growing Together's inception, the farmers have taught us as much as we did them about food, agriculture, and marketing, but when the Covid-19 pandemic hit, it was a scary and challenging time for all of us. And for our nonprofit, it was a crisis of community as much as anything else. While we are much more connected and interdependent than we could have ever thought, the brokenness of our global systems is amplified in times of crises, and therefore the impact is widespread. We have seen this in our healthcare system and in our economy, and it has and will continue to disproportionately impact the most vulnerable among us, especially communities of color, whom these systems were originally designed to exclude and exploit.

But in the spring of 2020, the Growing Together farmers, like so many farmers in our community and beyond, continued to plant seeds and transplants, tending the land with hope for what's to come. These farmers were not exempt from the fallout of these times. Many of them are elders in their communities and rely on support from their adult children—whose jobs were on hold or eliminated altogether. Some expressed concern and fear around the possibility of targeted racial violence. And as many of us can relate, the farmers have loved ones who are more susceptible to the virus, or are vulnerable themselves.

It is true that in fear, for humanity and for our fragile earth, we forget how deeply connected we are to one another and to all gifts of Creation. In fear, we build walls that keep us self-important, anxious, and isolated. All this displacement creates a real sense of who's in and who's out, who's right and who's wrong, and the boundaries between us become places of hatred, otherness, and sometimes violence.

But how many of us have had an unexpected, extraordinary encounter with someone at an unlikely time or place, butting up against a border of some kind, an ethnicity, religion, nationality, political perspective, and something small happens, and a hard separation is softened, or possibly wanes altogether, and new discoveries about oneself and another are found there? This is how a border can be sacred.

I heard professor and author Brené Brown once say that it's hard to hate someone up close—and painfully, beautifully, unpredictably . . . it's true. Every Saturday morning at a local farmers market in West Nashville, Nepali-speaking farmers sell their produce to a primarily English-speaking customer base. And the resilience of these humans, on both sides of the table, stands out. When the language barrier makes it impossible to ask a clear question or make an order, the vegetables themselves—perhaps red bok choy or the Nepalese greens called *saag* or even a prepared jar of *achaar*—can become words and points of connection between two people, with everyone gesturing and smiling.

If there is anything my work with poor communities over the last twelve years has taught me, it's that the borders and boundaries between us are also often places of hope, longing, discovery, and possibility. Food has a powerful way of highlighting difference, yet in many situations, it is also often our first invitation. I've been told that who we eat with is who we humanize. And this is how food can break down barriers between us and plant seeds of belonging in their place.

Going Back to God

My friends Viki and Emily have often used a phrase I've loved; to speak of what happens when we die, they'll say we "go back to God." Even though I don't believe God is separate from us when we're alive and here on earth, I've always loved this phrase as I imagine that final surrender to the Love who made us. A total and complete reunion with that Love we may not be capable of in these earthly bodies, with our earthly distractions, differences, and desires.

No matter what, loss is woven into life. I once heard someone despairingly say that life is just a collection of losses, and I remember feeling some sadness at the glass-half-empty way life was assessed in his depiction. I am learning in my life, in this time more acutely than ever, how much healing requires enormous surrender. Facing death, I am dancing with the despairing likelihood that my life will be much shorter than I want.

This is a beautiful piece of verse I have nearly obsessed over for the last decade, first introduced to me in a staff meeting at the Food Project by my friend and former co-worker Brooke. The imagery is so rich, and the writing so visceral and complete.

All will come again into its strength:
the fields undivided, the waters undammed,
the trees towering and the walls built low.
And in the valleys, people as strong
and varied as the land.

And no churches where God
is imprisoned and lamented
like a trapped and wounded animal.
The houses welcoming all who knock
and a sense of boundless offering
in all relations, and in you and me.

No yearning for an afterlife, no looking beyond,
no belittling of death,
but only longing for what belongs to us
and serving earth, lest we remain unused.

—RAINER MARIA RILKE[1]

To be restored to wholeness, to stay hopeful that healing—whatever that means to us—is possible: I believe in these things. I believe in it for me, for you, and for all humanity. And for this earth we have misused and abused. What strikes me when I read this is how small-minded we can be about one another, with our walls and our wants. How narrowly we conceive of God in our own image instead of remembering it's the other way around. But also it reminds me of the strength of God's enormous, infinite love for all of creation and the welcome we are all capable of.

When I think about my death and its effect on my young children in particular, I want them to imagine me going back to God, the source of Love that will hold them in their grief, that will continue to connect me to them, even in my death. I pray people do not tell them I'm in a better place, or that this is God's will or God's timing, or that everything happens for a reason. I have seen in my years of ministry how these theological claims have harmed so many in the throes of loss. I want them to build a capacity to embrace this sadness as the sadness it is, or as Rilke urges, "no belittling of death."

As I consider this brilliant poem and its deep meaning, I think about how my purpose may be the same in death as it continues to be in life—surrendering to the hope that our weaknesses can be made strong, that what is broken can be made whole.

That Hard Way

Robbie and I had been engaged for six months when he turned on some Quinn family home videos from his childhood that he had converted from Super 8 film to DVD. We put in the first disk to find his very first swim lesson fully recorded. Three-year-old Robbie with a styrofoam "bubble" belted to his middle, holding the hand of his swim teacher in the pool. After a few seconds of the video clip, another child swims into the frame, and we realized it's me! And my cousin Margo! And his sister Katy!

We couldn't believe the coincidence, as our families didn't know each other at all until more than a decade later, in 1995, when we met at Woodmont Christian Church. Robbie posted the video to YouTube, calling it our first date.

Our more than ten years of marriage have felt pretty charmed. Five pregnancies and two stunning children. Brokenhearted sorrow and wordless joy. Our exhausting jobs that have provided deeply meaningful work. Bills we've struggled to pay, and times we could give our money away. Daily laughter and nightly foot rubs. Unknowable numbers of nearly finished crossword puzzles, loads of cloth diapers washing at midnight, and huge green salads for dinner. A gazillion hands of gin rummy with what I've always hoped would be a never-ending scorecard in which I am always a little ahead.

So I am thinking this early morning about the miracle of love and how healing love with Robbie has been and continues to be for me. I know that marriage is not a safe or genuine place for everyone, and that many people have harmed and been harmed in their most intimate relationships. But our marriage has been a source of unconditional love and deep liberation for both of us, and as we pummel headfirst into a heartbreaking cancer diagnosis together, we have now entered into a time that is not ordinary, not what we wanted or expected, but together with God, we know we can show up for it.

Years ago my friend Viki shared a profound selection with me by the feminist poet Adrienne Rich, who wrote:

> An honorable human relationship—that is, one in which two people have the right to use the word "love"—is a process, delicate, violent, often terrifying to both persons involved, a process of refining the truths they can tell each other. It is important to do this because it breaks down human self-delusion and isolation. It is important to do this because in so doing we do justice to our own complexity. It is important to do this because we can count on so few people to go that hard way with us.[1]

We did not know, when we married, that we would face such an enormous, devastating loss. These days are full of doctors' appointments, correspondence, planning, and so many other details I cannot manage or keep up with. I feel such gratitude for Robbie and his ability to keep everything moving forward with so much love, flexibility, care, and genuine kindness. It is so fun to be with him, to be beside him, to be together with him. I love my life so much. There is literally nothing I would change about it, just to have more of it. And what a gift to feel that way. To love and be loved—I feel this love, and it's even greater than I can imagine. How does it come to be?

Somewhere along the way I became so wired for productivity and our schedule and the timeline—and controlling so much of that—but I believe I squeezed joy out of the moments that could've held more joy. It was ours for us to take. I have a lot of compassion and understanding for myself in these reflections, but I do also carry regret. It can be true to hold two things at once: gratitude and regret.

Living in this world, we encounter so much pain, and I am learning we have to be willing not only to face the pain but to embrace it, let it wash over us, let it move through us. The hope of heaven—or the promise that the love we feel will reunite with the Love who made us—keeps us from despair while we are alive, but does it also keep us from grieving? We say things like "All will be well," but does it rob the one who is in loss from facing her pain? Does volleying the pain away with these platitudes cheapen another's experience? I don't say this because people say the wrong thing or have offended me. If anything, I personally feel more held and loved and seen through this cancer than I can possibly express. This is a more general observation on our culture and what we make room for and what we don't.

I weep for the years that I will not be alive for my children growing up. I weep for the mixed-up conversations that hold court in my mind—a cognitive mix of beauty, heartbreak, memory, and still some amazing thoughts of my own exclamation! I have loved deeply. I will mourn for my early death. But I recognize this is fading, and will fade, and for all of us, that blessing brightly lit, will find its way to a close. Will it be quiet? Will it be peaceful? Will it rage?

Inside All This Heartache

When I was in the fourth grade, our class did a deep dive into Tennessee history. As part of the study, we spent awhile on the rich musical traditions of my hometown, Nashville. We were given an assignment to compose an original song about a subject of our choice. One lucky student's song would be chosen and performed by Layng Martine, Jr., a well-known songwriter in town, who is also a close family friend. The project would culminate in a field trip to the Country Music Hall of Fame, where the selected song would be performed live by Layng himself.

Since my dad was a songwriter, he had a modest recording studio in the basement of our home. So he and I worked up a rendition of my song, "We're on Our Way to Disney World," and set the masterpiece to music. I was secretly confident that Layng would pick my song and perform it in front of the rest of the fourth grade, but instead he picked Clementine Howard's song and sang it from the stage. Clementine was my friend, and her famous songwriting dad Harlan Howard had penned legendary hits like "I Fall to Pieces" and "I've Got a Tiger by the Tail." Of course Layng chose Clemmy's song!

My dad's songs have been such a formative part of my own identity. He started writing songs and playing music at a young age. He tells a story about a special gift his mother gave him—his first guitar. It was soon after his own father died of cancer at the age of forty-eight. My dad was only sixteen years old at the time, and from what I understand, my grandfather died in their home in agonizing, audible pain. I lament not knowing my paternal grandfather or even how to refer to him. To my brothers and me, he never had a grandfather name.

I've always sensed my dad has carried with him a grief that he cannot shake about losing his dad at such a young age. His deep faith in God and his masterful songwriting have no doubt been a balm for his broken heart for more than fifty years. I know my mom's love has helped too. As I've gotten older, I've noticed how some of the funniest people in my life also carry with them a lot of sadness, and I think my dad fits the bill.

But I did have the enormous pleasure of knowing my paternal grandmother, Vivian, very well, and I treasure the memories I have with her—her pure white bars of Ivory soap, her ability to wallop anyone in Scrabble, the way she'd take out her dentures for my brother Roy and me when we were good, and her enormous sunglasses with the side panels that she wore over her regular glasses. My dad is the fourth and youngest child in his family; his siblings are twelve, eleven, and ten years older than he is. A few years before she died, I asked my grandmother why there was a big gap in years before having my dad. She explained to me that my grandfather's alcoholism had been hard on their family in those early years of raising their babies. After he got sober, they wanted to try for one more child, and it was my dad. I remember marveling at her honesty and considering how truly miraculous it was that my dad had been born at all!

But grief. We can name it and face it, but it never leaves a person, and that sadness even trickles into the next generation and then the next. How has my father's grief influenced my life? How will my own grief influence my children's lives? And how will my children's grief influence the rest of theirs? Will the adults surrounding them be able to recognize it and let it be what it is? I am heartened by the human miracle that people are capable of holding enormous suffering, even while finding much joy in life. It's like the songwriter Shawn Colvin sings in her song "Trouble": "this world's a blessing and a beast, every day."

In the years when our globe was forced to grapple with suffering and death in the pandemic, there was also so much loss in my family. My gorgeous aunt Kathleen—my mom's only sister—died of cancer, after a six-year battle. One of her sons, my cousin Pat, recently visited me for an overnight stay at our house. The next morning he said he'd just woken up from a dream about her. He was smiling through a face full of tears and telling me how close he felt to her when he had those dreams.

After that, I had the honor of sitting with Kirke, Margo's dad, who'd entered hospice at the end of his battle with cancer. He was living his final days, and I can't find the words for the respect I feel for him in that most vulnerable time. I got to climb up onto the bed next to him while he was going in and out of sleep. We talked about cancer and heaven and my dad, whom he'd known all his life. In addition to getting weepy about my dad, Kirke was mentioning loved ones who had already died, as if they were in his presence. His hospice nurse told us that sometimes the one dying will name deceased loved ones, or even imagine they are in the room with them. Margo was there that day, and we talked about this kind of communion with these ancestor angels—the hard leaving and the slow entrance into what is to come. It's so much like birth, but the labor is different.

A lot of people die unexpectedly, and tragically there is no time for them or their loved ones to process what they will lose but haven't lost yet. I have thought often about how difficult it is to have a terminal illness, but what a gift it is to have this time to do my best to align my days with what is important to me. I'm not trying to gild the lily here—I hate this cancer. But for me, if I'm going to go out, I'd like to be prepared, and I do believe the way my diagnosis was detected affords me the time. What can I say, I've always been a planner! As I sort through my own grief and these generations of sorrow, I feel grateful to have a community of friends and family. I am finding nourishment as I meditate on my own death, and unbelievably, what I hear when I get quiet and listen is actually a song, crafted inside all this heartache.

Spinning in infinity

May the Road Rise to Meet You

I had a friend in Nicaragua named Juan Victor. He was twenty years old and the grandson of Martha, the woman I lived with. Juan's father had died by suicide eleven years before, and Juan's mother didn't provide basic things most parents provide for their children—clothes, food, nurturing. But he had a lot of cousins to pass his time with, and Martha fed him every day in exchange for help around the house and with the baby. Juan has some form of developmental disability, though it's not clear to me whether it's ever been given a name. I do know there were never enough resources to keep him in school. He didn't speak in sentences but used only single words, and since I spoke in single words too, we found ourselves together much of the time. And our sparse vocabulary was not all we had in common: like me, he had a younger brother named Roy.

In Central America, the Spanish term for speed bump is *policía acostado*, which translates to "a police officer laid down." It is one of those names for things that are so perfectly appropriate, and every time we drove over one, I would say *policía acostado* out loud and picture a big body thrown across the road to slow us down, like someone watching for us for when we're not watching for ourselves.

The extended family I lived with had turned the entire end of a dirt road into a compound of homes, in one of Managua's poorest neighborhoods. They truly lived in community—one long hose connecting all the water, one web of extension cords providing all the electricity. When the group of us met outside in the early mornings for our very slow walk, Juan usually came along. He liked to walk by my side, which I loved because it excused me from having to say too much so early, and because he was my favorite. He and I only used words occasionally, and whenever it was time to cross a street, he stopped me on the sidewalk and stepped out into the road to check for cars. When it was safe, he would give a strong nod and grab my hand. Being with him was like being with my child and my parent at the same time—someone I was watching out for, someone watching out for me.

In the evenings, when I returned home from my office, Juan was always sitting on our stoop watching, waiting. He'd quickly say a few indecipherable words to me in English and then bury his head into the collar of his shirt with a smile, flushed with embarrassment. This was the one thing I could count on in my daily life there: the water might or might not run, the electricity might or might not work, but when I reached home, Juan would be on the stoop, with his smile.

One night Juan's flip-flops got stolen—his only pair of shoes—and so he didn't meet us for our walk the next morning. I wanted to buy him new ones, because he's my friend and because I could. But what I wish I could've done is thrown my body across the hard road he walked, a road built of poverty, suicide, disability. A road built of never enough and the kinds of hard bumps that didn't protect him but kept him perpetually in danger.

But I couldn't do that, because how do we do that? I just let the road rise to meet me in this sweetest boy sitting on the edge of our stoop each night, and I learned from him, because he was slowing me and he was showing me. I don't know how he learned how to step out into the road like he did, but he did it like that's just what we do for each other—just lay our bodies down.

The Salmon

XXIX[1]

Silent friend of many distances, feel
how your breath enlarges all of space.
Let your presence ring out like a bell
into the night. What feeds upon your face

grows mighty from the nourishment thus offered.
Move through transformation, out and in.
What is the deepest loss that you have suffered?
If drinking is bitter, change yourself to wine.

In this immeasurable darkness, be the power
that rounds your senses in their magic ring,
the sense of their mysterious encounter.

And if the earthly no longer knows your name,
whisper to the silent earth: I'm flowing.
To the flashing water say: I am.

—RAINER MARIA RILKE, *The Sonnets to Orpheus*, II, 29

Our first Christmas after my diagnosis was so special—slow, an abundance of family time, a dim sweetness to the hours at home—although it was bookended by a couple of very intense headaches. The first of them resulted in a mild but lengthy seizure, and the second sent me to the hospital for an overnight stay and some strong intravenous medicines. My reading comprehension was gone entirely, and my field of vision was getting further compromised. My blood counts were too low to restart chemo, and I made the decision to discontinue Optune, the head device treatment I had been wearing faithfully for the previous three months. Instead I tried additional medications to try to mitigate any more symptoms. My recent MRI scans showed possible new tumor growth, although that couldn't be confirmed for another few weeks. It just seemed like we had not had a lot of good medical news in a while, and that had me feeling pretty down.

After the seizure, and with the MRIs showing potential new tumor growth, it seemed right to keep facing what is devastatingly true about glioblastoma and its very poor prognosis. I fear my death will come sooner than I first envisioned, although I fervently hope and pray that my intuition is wrong. There are going to be some bad days, and so I am trying to savor the good ones, and I believe there are still many of them ahead.

But my sadness overwhelms me today. And the truth is that I am so scared to die. I want to be strong and enter into all this gracefully, but I am afraid. My life has been so charmed and wonderful, filled with miracles—deep friendships, incredible parents, hilarious siblings, two children, my loving spouse, the most awesome family I married into, meaningful work—not to mention I have seen the Indigo Girls in concert nearly fifty times!

When I had babies, I remember the postpartum panic that

would come over me. Usually my imagination would take me to an anxious headspace in which my husband died tragically and I was left to raise our children without him. I've similarly panicked about one of them dying young too. I've believed myself to be strong enough to be courageous and capable of facing all that pain and loss. But I never really conceived that I could be the one to die young, and this is such an out-of-my-control loss. I cannot stop its progression or ultimately change it. So I am thinking about what I *can* do in this time. My hospital stay and symptoms gave me a sense of urgency to make a so-called bucket list and set priorities for the ways I'm spending my time. I've considered how our lifestyle may have to get a little smaller in order to focus our time, to let every visit count, to find the bravery to have hard conversations, because I realize I don't have a lot of time or a lot to lose. I guess this is the essence of my bucket list.

I asked my friend John if he would lead my funeral and do my eulogy. He said absolutely, he would be honored, but only on the condition that I would do his. What an incredible answer! And what an incredible friend. And my friend Bonnie introduced me to a local nonprofit called Larkspur Conservation here in Tennessee that supports the process of natural burial.[2]

Having been one of the family members who got to sit with my cousin Kirke before he died, I've been marveling at how one day we're holding the hand of a living, breathing beloved body and only a few days later scattering the ashes from that very flesh and bone into eternity. The veil between life and death is thin.

My friend Scott has been bringing me communion to my bedroom. Before becoming ordained as an Episcopal priest, he had a ministry as a hospice chaplain, so he's very comfortable sitting with folks living with terminal illnesses and thus talking about dying, transition, eternity, angels, and the fears on my mind right now. It is such a gift to be in the presence of those who can hold the sadness and the fear and not try to take it away but just meet me there inside it.

The Rilke passage above confounds me. I take away from it that struggle and deep loss can produce strength, and while I understand and feel that, I simultaneously find it so problematic. I do not like the theological claims of suffering being salvific. For example, the last line of Saint Francis's brilliant prayer is "for it is in dying we are born to eternal life."[3] What does it mean? Theologically I struggle with this, yet I also find comfort in it. There is a passage in the gospels where Jesus says, "I came so that everyone would have life, and have it in its fullest" (John 10:10). What does it mean to have life and have it in its fullest? There has been, in my interpretation, so much maligned, antigospel translation of this passage. Living life to the fullest is certainly not about accumulation or quantities—money, friendships, homes, even opportunities. I imagine the "fullest" here is about living deeply, with intention, with purpose aligned within the essence of God's call and hope for us, which is really to deeply love and let ourselves be loved. As I think and feel my way through whatever remaining time I have, I've been reflecting on these questions and asking God to guide me toward answers. I lie awake in my bed at night, and like the disciple Thomas, I pray, *I believe! But forgive my unbelief!*

Our family is working through these questions in different ways. We've had the remarkable privilege of working with a psychologist to give our children additional context around my cancer diagnosis and some space to process the many emotions that accompany it. In an appointment, my six-year-old son, Thomas, shared quite a bit with Dr. Herrington about my cancer. She asked him to draw a heart and write down words inside the heart of what needed extra special love. His list included "fish caught in nets" (and not released), Christmas trees that were chopped down for the holidays, and his family. She then gave him a Band-Aid to put on top of one of those concerns in need of special love right now, so he put it on top of the word *family*.

We finished up our session by reading an incredible children's book our friend Kendall sent us called *The Invisible String*.[4] It's a story about loss, and how people remain connected in their love even after separation or death. Since that appointment, Thomas and I have been using a hand gesture of tugging on the invisible string that connects us to one another in love.

My mom recently told me a wonderful story about her own version of the invisible string. She takes a bike ride every morning on Jekyll Island, where she lives. As she rides, she silently talks to her deceased loved ones, like a long telephone call with an invisible cord. First she calls her mother and then her father and then her sister Kathleen. Then she moves on to God, and then Jesus. And then, to wrap it up, she asks Jesus if he could put Kathleen back on the line. Because I guess that's how she lives to the fullest!

Part of my process lately has been to open myself to meditation. In one meditation, I met a huge salmon—female and strong. She met me at the edge of the water and said, "I got you, follow me," and all I had to do was hold on to her tail and follow. I didn't have to fix anything or worry about anything, all I had to do was hold on. She swam us down and down in the water to a place called the chamber of gifts. I was supposed to pick a gift, and then I realized that *she was the gift*! But I couldn't take her with me. She told me I could call on her anytime, and she would meet me in our place at the edge of the water, and that she will always, always know how to go back, to find me, to meet me there. That friend who can help me whisper to the flashing water, I am.

Larkspur

Emotionally, one of the most difficult parts of planning for my death has been making decisions that have future consequences after I am gone from this physical world—like investing in a burial plot now, with room for Robbie beside my body in the ground. But what if he goes on to marry again, and he gets a blessed forty-plus years in a second marriage? I bawl my eyes out when I think of it, even as I want this happiness for him. How can I make plans now that give me a sense of peace for a future none of us can see or know? And how can this planning answer the questions we'd like answered now, without locking anyone into something that will be too difficult or painful to undo in some future time?

For me, facing my own mortality has changed my thoughts on what I believe about the body in death, how we memorialize the dead, and other cultural norms of engaging with the end of human life. I always naïvely assumed I would be cremated on the occasion of my death—as an old woman—and my ashes tossed into the ocean at our beloved Jekyll Island, as my way to reconnect my dead body with the living earth. I have imagined the salt water of the ocean like the amniotic fluid at birth. We are water to water and dust to dust. But since I'm dying young, and I have young children whom I want to help shepherd and make sense of this senseless illness for, I have reconsidered how important it is for them to have a physical place to visit after I have passed from this living world and their physical grasp.

This has led me to learn more about in-ground burial options, which brings me back to Larkspur Conservation, that Bonnie told me about. The larkspur itself—for which the preserve is aptly named—is a type of plant called a spring ephemeral; it pops up from the ground in woodland ecosystems, has a very short bloom life, and then dies. The larkspur does not linger, its beauty emerges quickly and leaves quickly. It's a quick flush of a purple blossom, and then it's gone. This whole process reflects the ephemeral quality of a person's life.

Robbie, my mom, my cousin Margo, and I recently visited the preserve when all the larkspur were in bloom everywhere. As we walked along both the woodland trails and the meadow trails, gorgeous purple flowering larkspur lined the ground. The timing didn't feel like something we could have planned! Walking through the preserve, it became clear that the design and layout of the physical site is so intentional, reflecting elements of the natural world around us. Even the visitors' map is a watercolor rendering of the preserve, with an ephemeral quality, wet and impermanent.

We brushed by purple coneflower, pawpaw, violets galore, trillium, a turtle shell now home to a colony of fire ants, buttercups, and bullfrogs. The trees had all leafed out. On our walk, we found crinoids from millennia past, geodes, arrowheads—all evidence of cycles of former life and subsequent death. As I walked the grounds, I had a real sense I could never feel alone here. Taking my mom on this visit was so important to me. What was it like for her to accompany me on a tour like that? It was just another difficult aspect of the reality of this diagnosis she is facing with a lot of faith and strength. We were all in and out of tears as we walked the trails, at our different times and with our different thoughts. My sadness and my gratitude are so entwined and impossible to pull apart. I was crying because I hated the walk and also because I loved it. As Whitman poetically acknowledged, we contain multitudes. I feel that more now than I have felt at any other point in my life.

Margo has been an important part of these decisions about my burial. As an adult, she has been a doula in many births and has recently enrolled in a program to be certified as an end-of-life doula. Margo's particular capacity for accompanying people in death and loss has been honed because she herself has experienced so much personal loss. And she has had the special but difficult role of sitting with those as they pass from this life to whatever comes next. It is a deep calling she has been living for more than a decade, and it's incredible to watch and listen to how she is pulling together her experiences with what life is asking of her now. I see how this is the coming together of a person's vocation. I don't know that this was ever her life's plan, but I am struck by how skilled, motivated, confident, and comfortable she is entering into this role and these conversations. I watch in awe as she accepts and compassionately passes along the gifts within herself that have cultivated and catalyzed this next part of her journey.

Part of Margo's process has been weaving on her floor loom in the night, after her three children and husband are long asleep. She has woven me a burial shroud. It is soft and gorgeous. Can you imagine this gift—to be robed in something handmade, designed with such care? The time and intention—her fingers having slid across every thread of cotton warp and cotton weft, as she pulls together this offering, unlike any other I have received. I won't even really "be" there to receive it, and yet how could it be anyone else's but mine if it wraps me in my death and it's buried in the ground with me and only me? Into this shroud, I imagine her weaving past, present, and future prayers—not just for the dying but for all of us trying to make sense of death coming too soon.

When we memorialize someone at their funeral or in their eulogy, we are pulling together all those strands into a woven whole by which we can tell the story of the life they lived. I love the strands of the shroud as that image, and as the covering over the body as it meets its final resting place, settling into the cycle that is dust to dust. We are fleeting, stunning, song-filled, tender, determined, strung together into an imperfect but woven whole. We are the trillium, spicebush, monarch, turtle shell, fire ant, wild dogwood, redbud, mayapple, goldenseal, bluebell. And the ephemeral larkspur, whose incredible strength is like our fleeting, willful, miraculous lives. You show us how to live. You show us how to die. Can you show us the way beyond death?

Hale, Hallowed, Holy

I'm thinking about what it felt like to sit at the kitchen table of my childhood home. When we were young, my brother Roy invented a game that became so beloved in our family. Thinking on it now, I find myself in a fit of nostalgia; it's the kind of happy memory I love to go back to. At dinnertime, my mom, dad, brother, and I would be eating at the kitchen table, and at some point during the meal, Roy would announce he needed to use the bathroom and leave the table. But instead of going to the bathroom, he would quietly crawl back into the kitchen on the floor, slide under the table, and kiss each one of us on the knee. And our mom would say, "Oh! It's the kissing bug!" with a joy in her voice I can still hear. "He's come to visit us again!"

Sitting above the table and making eyes with my parents, I loved to be part of this world with my whole family. It evoked feelings of fullness that as an adult, I now associate with feelings of belonging to a place or to a person or to a group of people. After the kissing bug made his last round of kisses, my brother would slide out in secret and walk back into the kitchen a moment later, as if he'd just washed his hands in the bathroom sink. "Roy, you always miss the kissing bug!" our dad would say. "He seems to come every time you're gone!" And Roy would climb into his chair at the kitchen table and try not to smile. To make a place for this kind of loving pretending—what a gift this was to us as children. As a parent to two young children now, I am reminded constantly of how important it is to climb into their world.

At the Food Project, we had a volunteer named John who worked in our kitchen every Tuesday and most Wednesdays. He had been locked up when he was seventeen for auto theft with a weapon. Several years later, he was trying to reenter a society that had never claimed him in the first place. John told me once about the first day he visited the kitchen. At the time, he was living in a halfway house after leaving prison. He came to volunteer, and immediately my friend and co-worker Anne set him up at a counter with four dozen eggs, some stale bread, an enormous bowl, a whisk, and a recipe: bread pudding for a hundred.

Months later, he recounted the story of his first day to me. Nobody had ever before in his entire life, he said, talked to him like he was capable of doing anything but break stuff and get in trouble. Never before had someone greeted him as though he was capable of even a simple task, like whisking eggs. At home, his mom had always told him: "Stay away from that. Get outta here. You'll break something." But so much in his life was already broken. John said that that first day, he'd wanted a cleaning task, something he'd done in prison, something simple and solo, something that wouldn't require him to speak to anybody or be known by anyone. But long after his period of mandatory community service was over, he still volunteered with us every week. It was not the food that brought him back, or the work. It was Anne. And Sarah and Grace, and all the others in our kitchen who provide what we all need most: kinship. Spending time getting to know others, and spending time letting ourselves be known.

The Kentucky writer Wendell Berry reflects on healing in his book *The Art of the Commonplace:*

> The concept of health is rooted in the concept of wholeness. To be healthy is to be whole. The word *health* belongs to a family of words . . . : *heal, whole, wholesome, hale, hallowed, holy.* . . . If the body is healthy, then it is whole. . . . The body cannot be whole alone. People cannot be whole alone. . . . Healing is impossible in loneliness; it is the opposite of loneliness.[1]

At one of our weekly meal sites called Trinity Community Ministry, neighbors gather in a large church basement to share a meal. There are tablecloths, real plates, real silverware, and flowers for the center of the tables. The assembled Tuesday-night crowd is a mix of working people and retirees, single moms and their children, lonely people, tired people, young people and old.

The meal is shared family style, and everyone wears a name tag. One Trinity neighbor named Ms. Johnnie had been regularly attending on Tuesday nights, and one evening she showed up with a black-and-white composition notebook. She opened to the first page, which held a couple of name tags from previous weeks: MS. JOHNNIE, MS. JOHNNIE. She opened to the second page, more name tags: MS. JOHNNIE, MS. JOHNNIE. And as she flipped through the leaves of her composition notebook, every name tag was saved there—her treasured memories of what it felt like to know and be known.

Perhaps Johnnie and John, like my brother Roy, might've played the kissing bug too at their family's kitchen tables. They have shown me much about the opposites to loneliness, over stale bread, a whisk, a dinner table, a name tag, and a hallowed place. If only we could all be known in such a way.

Normal Days

After the Covid-19 pandemic started, our two children began wearing our T-shirts to sleep in. With virtual school, we parents were "choosing our battles" and became very lax about things like getting dressed for school in the mornings. One day our daughter silently mouthed to me during class, "Mom, can I turn off my video to put on some pants?" Anyway, most days our kids had been staying in the oversize T-shirts they slept in the night before. The T-shirt Lulah wore one day was a faded chocolate-brown color—nearly twenty years old, I bet—from our beloved church camp here in Tennessee. On the back of the shirt there is a passage of writing by Mary Jean Irion, and in this new reality for me and my family, the words offered new perspective, truth, and beauty:

> Normal day, let me be aware of the treasure you are. Let me learn from you, love you, bless you before you depart. Let me not pass you by in quest of some rare and perfect tomorrow. Let me hold you while I may, for it may not always be so. One day I shall dig my nails into the earth, or bury my

face in the pillow, or stretch myself taut, or raise my hands
to the sky and want, more than all the world, your return.[1]

A normal day is rarely the kind of passage of time we consider
celebrating, I guess until something devastating happens and
threatens it, and then, as Mary Jean Irion writes, we wish, more
than anything, for its return. In life it seems like we are either
crushingly unaware of the gifts of "ordinary" time, or we are aching to get back to that kind of time that is out of reach. As awake as
we try to live, we still miss the gifts. Perhaps this is part of the
human experience—always a longing for what eludes us.

During my radiation and chemo treatments, I found a rhythm,
with the help of my husband and our families, and I genuinely
cherished every smile and good morning and joke I received from
the incredible staff at Vanderbilt I encountered every day. But I
was also very tired and generally overwhelmed and worn down. I
think about that "normal day" that is now beyond my grasp—one
in which I make breakfast for my family, start a load of laundry,
scroll the headlines while sipping coffee, drive myself to the job I
love, make dinner, clean off the kitchen counter that is like a mag-
net for stuff, read my children bedtime stories, wash my own hair,
and change our sheets. The list of these ordinary things goes on.

I guess none of us have been living in "normal" times, given
we were all coping through a global pandemic, so I'm not sure
whether this passage offers you all a fitting point of reflection right
now. Earlier in the summer of 2020, maybe in June, before any
symptoms of my brain tumor set in, I remember saying to a couple of my closest co-worker friends, "Twenty-twenty, man, the
hits keep coming! Surely this is it, right?" without knowing of
course that in a matter of weeks my new "normal day" would be
navigating how to manage living with brain cancer.

Even in this new normal, I love my life so much. I love what it has been, and truthfully I love what it is now, even though I spend a lot of time feeling very, very sad. What else are we to do but surrender and accept what is in front of us? The alternative is either delusion or despair. However many days I have left, it's too few to live in denial or inconsolable anger. So my new normal day now includes more deeply felt sadness. I think that the same is true for the people who love me—a new and deep sadness that cannot be pushed away or covered up. I do not know what there is for us to do but embrace the sadness.

Wherever these words find you today—paying bills, rolling trash bins down the driveway, helping your kids with homework, going on a walk, folding clothes, brushing your child's hair—I hope this normal day holds you as only this day can.

A Loose Hold

The dishes that we received as wedding gifts are a set of beautifully handmade pottery that we love. We joke about the pottery
often because each dish must be hand-washed. I vividly remember when our two children were very young and the daily work at
home was abundant. There was this one night Robbie and I were
blaming each other about the buildup of dirty dishes in the kitchen,
and he turned to me and said, "It's just that sometimes I come to
our sink full of dirty dishes, and I wonder whether anything we
have can go in the dishwasher?" And then we laughed, and it broke
the marital tension in an instant.

I love the story of our dishes. When we were considering a
wedding registry, I pulled out a stack of six small dessert plates in
six different colors. I'd bought them in Vermont years before. I
flipped over a plate and saw that they were handmade by someone
who signed their pots "R. Wood Studio." We looked online for
R. Wood Studio, and it turned out Rebecca Wood's fine pottery is
made in Athens, Georgia, where Robbie lived for seven years. A
few months later we visited R. Wood Studio together, which
turned out to be located only a block away from his old apart-

ment, and decided it would be the perfect place to register for our wedding.

Like any pottery that is used every day, many of the bowls and plates have cracked or chipped or broken altogether over the last ten years. All those meals! We hand-wash every piece and even fetch out the dirty ones a babysitter or relative unknowingly places into the dishwasher. Tonight I am thinking about what it will feel like for Robbie, on some distant day, when the last piece of our pottery cracks and gets tossed into the garbage bin. It's just another image I have when I find myself thinking about him here without me, bravely parenting our two sensitive children in a very scary world, helping them navigate this life that will include much suffering.

What will he think about while slogging solo through the hand-wash-only dishes? In times of overwhelm, will he resent my death? Will he feel so alone? Will he embrace his grief? Will he know how to cook dinner? Will he find some other bright companion when he is ready? What will she think of the handmade pottery?

The beautiful pottery is just one of many earthly treasures I think about starting to loosen myself from—the preciousness of all that I cherish in this physical life that I will not be able to take with me when I pass on from this to that. These treasures are not opulent and probably resemble things you may cherish as well: the wobbly clay pinch pots sculpted by chubby young hands; the pressed dried wildflowers stashed between the leaves of a book; postcards and photographs and letters I've saved; the crushed paper cup Christmas ornaments dangling from a pipe cleaner; the calligraphy and art my mother has made over the years. And not to be forgotten, the bottomless stash of gorgeous yarns I can no longer knit, and the heavy-laden bookshelves of words I have cherished but can no longer read.

I've been thinking about heaven constantly—what I believe about it and what I wonder about it. I have intellectualized heaven so much, but lately I am meditating almost daily on what it will be like to reunite with God without the earthly trappings that prevent full and profound communion.

I despair when I think about how, in my death, I will leave Robbie and our two children, whose bodies and voices I know as intimately as my own. I think about my physical separation from them, and it occurred to me that, in my death, I could reunite with the three babies we lost to miscarriage—one in 2013, one in 2015, and one in 2019. The nightmare of dying young and leaving my living family is softened a bit when I imagine the possibility that in heaven I might reunite with all this love I carried in my body but knew only partially. What will it be like to leave this and enter into that?

I dwell with grief. For me, this is the natural consequence of living with terminal cancer and meditating on all I love. Some may interpret this as hopelessness or a lack of faith on my part that I could live another decade. But the truth is, as much as I journey to heaven in my mind and imagine who I might be able to love on and hold, I also go to sleep picturing Lulah at her graduation from high school or marveling at Thomas starring in a high school theater production. I can articulate every detail of this imagined future in which I am alive for these far-off dreams, even as I meditate on my own death. Florence + the Machine have a song called "100 Years" with a chorus that concludes "Give me arms to pray with / Instead of ones that hold too tightly." I am holding both my hope and my grief together in the same hands. It is a loose hold, looser than I am accustomed to. My love is so much bigger than me.

Mermaid Avenue

As if

We recently spent the weekend with our friends Johnny and Deb at their farm in Mississippi, just off the Natchez Trace. Johnny is an old friend and mentor—we went to Bosnia together when I was in seminary. He's retired but was a beloved preacher in our denomination, and now a farmer. He has amassed some truly fabulous stories because of his vast travels and deep friendships across the globe. And for every story, he has increased in compassion too. I treasure our yearly visits and always leave Johnny and Deb's place feeling happy and more hopeful than when I arrived.

Typically when we visit High Hope Farm, I get to mow some fields on the tractor. Not this year because of my eyesight, but these parcels of land are no less known to me. A person can work out the knots in her mind spending a few solid hours on the tractor mowing a field. It is one of my favorite ways to pass the time, perhaps because I can visually see my progress as I go along, unlike so much other work in life.

At the farm, doing the daily chores is so pleasurable. Everything at High Hope is meticulously and intentionally cared for. The layout of the physical space so reflects the care with which

Johnny and Deb approach their work. The trees are mulched. The steer get moved to a new paddock of special grasses every day. The hay is neatly tucked into the barn for the winter. Fences are in great shape. At their farm, my family has worked the lambs, mucked the stalls, moved the steer, collected the eggs, clipped the herbs, and during one visit, watched a neighbor check on the beehives.

I am so drawn to this well-cared-for place and these daily practices. Doing these chores does not confuse the mind but smooths it out somehow. Johnny and Deb's farmwork is suffused in what I observe to be applied hope. They give to their land more than they take from it. They do not overgraze their fields or use chemical fertilizers or pesticides. They earn a decent wage, but they have made a conscientious choice—and make this choice daily—to trade in the fear-based economic methods of extraction for stewardship that recognizes how the health of their land is always connected to their own health and the health of their community.

It is not lost on me that the farm is called High Hope. For me, it is a thin place, a place where God's presence is easily felt and our love of God is freely expressed. The poet Maxine Kumin has a powerful line of writing I've been carrying around for nearly two decades: "It is important to act as if bearing witness matters."[1]

As if. There is a lot to those tiny two words. We have to practice what we hope for *as if* what we hope for might be possible. I thought about this so much while I was at the farm. We have to flex our muscles of imagination, and we have to keep flexing, for the bearing witness matters. The reason I know it matters is because the witness of so many people has mattered to me: the neighbor who picks up trash in our park, the school bus driver who slips extra food to the kids on her route, the donor who sends in her $5.15 donation each month, the dad who's coaching soccer for my uninterested nine-year-old and a gaggle of her friends, and anyone who was responsible enough to wear a mask during the height of the pandemic. Showing up like this requires effort, but more important it requires enormous faith, which I've been told is the substance of things hoped for, the evidence of which is not always seen.

My own mental anguish has, at times, found me in a real state of limiting belief and lack of faithful imagination. I think to myself that I won't live very long. I tell myself I don't have what it takes to keep going. My impairment and limitations overwhelm any sense of moving forward. For many of us, we don't dare to live into our imagination until something really bad happens—like a pandemic or the loss of something we loved, like a job or a friend. In loss, perhaps with less to lose, our imagination wakes up, and we find the courage to go toward something we previously thought wasn't within reach for us or for our community.

Staying hopeful in a really hard time can feel like such a daunting task. But breaking hope down into small acts, or small daily practices, makes staying faithful easier. The daunting thing becomes possible when approached little by little. Hope has to be not only imagined but practiced. We have to do the work of imagining what could be possible, then do our little part to make it real. A current example of this is how voting is an act of bearing witness. You mean my tiny vote could mean something in healing our deep societal wounds? Impossible! But during each major national election lately, we all reflect on how much every single vote matters.

For me, even writing down these words has been a practice of bearing witness. I think about how meaningless my tiny story is in the bigger picture of our lives. But in putting this out there anyway, I'm choosing to believe that bearing witness to both my sadness and my hope, in some small way matters. I know it matters to me.

Hugs and Kisses for the Journey

One morning recently our son, Thomas, plunked down into my lap so I could help him with his socks. While he was there, I kissed him on his sticky cheek and took a quick, deep drink of the smell of him. The skin behind his ear smelled both sweet and slightly acrid. My eyes welled up as the tears came, thinking about my children's bodies and the very physical, embodied work of mothering them. So much of a parent's love is expressed physically, at least during these young years—tucking in, snuggling up, washing hair, combing out tangles, wiping bottoms, humming songs. When I was a child, my mother taught me that whenever she'd squeeze my hand three times, she was telling me she loved me. My own children and I do the hand squeezing too, and I am so grateful there are a gazillion ways to express and receive love. I need a gazillion more.

One week we went hiking in the Blue Ridge Mountains to celebrate the completion of my first round of chemo and radiation. On our walks there, we picked up muscadines, buckeyes, and persimmons on the trails. The crush of wildflowers and sweet shrub scented the way. There were blackberry, rudbeckia, Queen Anne's lace, and goldenrod along every roadside. We heard forest birds calling and acorns falling, and the rush of the streams beside us. One morning we walked on a trail called Angel Falls toward a waterfall bearing the same name. My family walked in front of me while I lagged behind, and I saw Robbie up ahead flapping his arms as though they were the wings of an imaginary dragon our children had asked him to be. He has this unbelievable capacity for climbing into their world and staying there for a long time. As I continued to watch and walk and listen to their laughter, I thought to myself, Why me? Why did I get so lucky to love these particular people and to be loved by them? How did it come to be that these angels are the ones I walk alongside and get to call my family?

Oh, to love someone in the flesh! How do we even contain such love within us? I am so grateful for this embodied life and all the pleasure I have experienced being alive. It is of course also my body and its illness that will take me from this physical world and the people I love. It is our bodies that wear out, become frail, stop working, or become riddled with cancers. I have considered how dying young and dying while my kids are still young seems like a breach of the contract that I made when I chose to become a mom—to give myself to them—my strong body, my sound mind. To be both porch and porch light for their own bodies becoming. To be open-armed, open-hearted, and open-eyed to who they are.

When our kids were learning how to swim, I needed a special way to get them to leave the comfort of the edge of the pool. I told them, "Let me give you some hugs and kisses for the journey," and so we hugged and kissed and held each other, and then I backed up a modest twelve or eighteen inches, and like magic they pushed off from the edge and swam into my arms. The celebrations were epic!

All I want is to keep watching them grow up—my children, born of my flesh, birthed through my body. Can I offer them, while I am still here in this body, enough love for that impossible journey they will take—growing up without their mom? After I die, how will they find and feel my love? They won't be able to swim into my arms, or feel the three squeezes of my hand, or have hold of me in the ways they know me now. They will have me in memory and in spirit and in love. I guess they may not remember the physical feel of me, but I want them to know I will never forget theirs.

The Forest and the Clearing

I am thinking about Robbie tonight, and so many funny stories of life with him. There was the summer I flew to New Hampshire to visit him, where he was working at Dartmouth College. I arrived at the dorm room where he was living to find his bed made with a new-to-me twin sheet set bearing a scene from Prince Caspian from the *Chronicles of Narnia* series. There was my thirtieth birthday when he handed me a brown paper sack and inside was a knitted cowl—handmade by him—and I didn't even know he could knit! There was the time he used our good bread knife with a serrated blade to cut a two-by-four when he couldn't find a saw. And the time, when we had just started dating, and we were making dinner in his apartment. He asked me, "So do you know how to make soups and stuff?" I looked at him and said, "I'm like a *really* good cook." There was the time he spent four months' worth of groceries on Lizzo tickets for his little sister without talking to me first. And one of my faves—we were cleaning out a closet with luggage in it. He opened up a suitcase we hadn't used in a while, and inside he found a red Dot—the gummy candy. I watched him pick it out of the suitcase, dust it off, and pop it in his mouth.

The kids and I woke up sleepy one morning recently, slow and grumpy. As I came down the stairs, he handed me coffee and started singing "It's Beginning to Look a Lot Like Christmas." Another day he got our children pumped doing a song and dance in his jammies about how it's recycling week—our favorite week of the month. Miraculously we made it out the door to get to school on time, and he was the kind engine that got us there.

When we got married, our friend Viki officiated our wedding, and during the ceremony she referenced our wedding reading—a seven-part poem by Wendell Berry called "The Country of Marriage." In my fifteen years of officiating weddings, several of our closest friends have also used this Berry poem in their ceremonies. Here is part three of the poem:

> *Sometimes our life reminds me*
> *of a forest in which there is a graceful clearing*
> *and in that opening a house,*
> *an orchard and garden,*
> *comfortable shades, and flowers*
> *red and yellow in the sun, a pattern*
> *made in the light for the light to return to.*
> *The forest is mostly dark, its ways*
> *to be made anew day after day, the dark*
> *richer than the light and more blessed,*
> *provided we stay brave*
> *enough to keep going in.*

I understand this metaphor for marriage as both the clearing and a forest. When we marry, we think it will be a life in the clearing, but it is a lot of forest. It's pretty obvious to state it, but this cancer finds us in the darkest part of the forest. Darker than dark.

And in stress and fear and grief and the vast unknown, my spouse is bringing forward his absolute very best. I get so overwhelmed and frustrated with my limitations, and he quietly, patiently, lovingly comes to my side with all the kindness I imagine a person can muster.

When you marry someone, you cannot know how your years together will unfold. You cannot know the forest will contain so much loss or sadness or struggle. You cannot even know how many years you will have together. Not long ago I changed the words to the benediction I typically used at the conclusion of each wedding ceremony I officiated. I'd say, "Walk now, into whatever comes next, knowing that God who is love, is always, always walking with you." Isn't that all we can know about the unknowable future—that something will happen next, and the great benevolent Love who made us will not leave us?

While I was still relatively healthy, our dear friends Cari and Steve got married, and because of Covid precautions, there were only a few invited guests. Robbie and I had the supreme honor of being among them. I was officiating the ceremony and had prepared a homily for the service. When I got to the part where I would typically read the reflection, I could tell I would not be able to physically read it because I was having trouble seeing my notes. I motioned to Robbie from the altar and asked him to come forward, explaining to the guests that they were my words he'd be reading and that I'd recently been diagnosed with an illness that had affected my ability to read. Without pause, he grabbed my hand and held it and began reading the reflection, which referenced the themes of their wedding reading, the same as ours: "The Country of Marriage."

As I think about him doing that for Cari and Steve and for me, I think about how the forest really *is* richer and more blessed. He and I have spent so many of our married days in the clearing. Despite significant heartache and loss, our marriage has felt like an embarrassment of riches in a wide-open clearing. But we are in the forest now. I feel strangely grateful for the forest tonight, for its blessings, because we are together here, and we were brave today, and I believe we will be brave again tomorrow.

Without Dreams

One week in Nicaragua, I came home to my precious Nicaraguan family and the usual bustle of evening commotion: The kitchen was busy in dinner preparation, two-year-old Jeshua was running around in his sandals and cloth diaper, a soap opera was screaming from the television, a woman was selling rice pudding and yelling her price from the street, and all of us were hustling to pull the clothes down from the line before they got wet in the evening rain.

Back in the kitchen, huddled over the tiny stove, I was tasting Martha's soup with a spoon when Wendi, her adult daughter, told me she'd found a job—something she'd been looking for since I met her a few months before. Wendi was smiling, but Martha, who was making lemonade over a big plastic bowl, was not. I asked Wendi how she found the job, what she would be doing, where it was located in the city, which bus she would take. She answered the questions one by one and ended in quiet tears as she explained that the work was outside Managua, and she'd be moving three hours away to Chinandega to take the job.

At some point that same week, we inherited a gigantic cardboard box, and Jeshua and his nine-year-old cousin Ali rolled across the tile floor inside it with their four legs and two heads sticking out. The box had been crushed and flattened and had ceded any of its former shape and hard edges to the rough love of these little boys. Watching them roll around in it—stopping only for cement walls and so much laughter—would make anyone believe that lack of resources keeps people together, keeps people talking, keeps people in the same room to invent with wild imagination how to pass time.

When I was in Nicaragua, I received a lot of mail and email from friends and family who expressed a want to escape the excesses that life at home afforded. I totally get these sentiments and understand how attractive a simpler life often seems to those of us burdened by too much activity, choice, responsibility, or stuff. From a distance, those of us with plenty can reach a conclusion that poverty somehow equals a simplicity or a basic happiness that we who are comfortable are not capable of living.

But I don't think anything about my Nicaraguan family's life was simple, certainly not their poverty. While we were watching the cardboard box game and eating dinner, I asked Martha how she felt about Wendi's new job. Her whole body held worry, grooves of heartache worn into her face like tattoos, like marks that would never leave her. She kept her eyes on her grandsons in the box and slowly listed the things she hoped to be able to give her daughter before she left—a big bag of oatmeal from Price-mart, a couple of pounds of rice, some beans, a few dollars' worth of minutes on her cellphone—but she didn't know if she would be able to do it.

Poverty busts up families, often at the cost of draining their one greatest resource—each other. Chronic poverty ruins dreams or replaces the human capacity for dreaming with something sadder than I have the words to describe. Most days it felt like I was living among people who did not dream, who had not been taught to dream, who could not afford to dream. Or in Wendi's case, whose one dream of raising her son, Jeshua, came at the cost of living apart from him, at the cost of missing his most precious growing-up years.

I watched the boys in the cardboard box until it was time for all of us to go to bed. Wendi called Jeshua into her arms, and he gave her the biggest, wettest kiss on her eye. I went into my room and washed my face with soap that cost at least three times as much as the combined cost of those modest things Martha wanted to send with Wendi. And when I turned out the light and pulled the sheet over my tired body, I cried for I don't know how long. As the reality of their poverty unfolded, I prayed every day that my tears weren't ones that paralyzed but ones that galvanized. That there are many people living without dreams only made me want to work harder for my own—the impossible ones that would establish economic justice—ones that require a few of us having a lot less and a lot of us having a little more. I am in bed so often now with tears from what seems at times like bottomless sadness. I listen to news updates from cycles of stories about corruption, partisanship, environmental negligence, endemic racism, and greed. I know that I have to keep holding on to what I wish were true about myself and this world, even when I can no longer do the kind of work I used to, and hope that those I know and those I will never know can carry their own impossible dreams too.

In You and Among You

It's becoming harder and harder for me to think and write, and I'm so tired that it's been awhile since I've had the strength to share any updates with anyone. A recent MRI showed new tumor growth—enough progression over the last few months that the doctors took me out of the clinical trial I started in Birmingham. I was devastated about this and hoped we would be shown the next right thing.

The tumor board at the University of Alabama, Birmingham, shared a list of next steps that includes another possible surgery to debulk the tenacious tumor, along with a potential option for another clinical trial. My doctors increased one of the antiseizure medications, which mitigates headaches too. It seems like this is a stage of decision-making in which we stay mindful of quality of life as we consider any other treatment options available.

The progression of the cancer and the barreling down of these momentous personal decisions feel so fast and so surreal. I am crying so much, and in addition to the daily tears, other aspects of our family life gradually convey changes in our day-to-day. I frequently get debilitating headaches that take me down, often accompanied by mild seizures. My children witness them. During the seizures, I am "awake," but I can't talk. It's so frustrating for me. And even in nonseizure times, I can't read or support Thomas with his sight-words or help Lulah with her Girl Scout cookie order. I get very turned around and mixed up when navigating the interior of our house, even though I know it like the back of my hand. And I can write all day, then write some more, but I can't read a single word back to myself without Siri's help. I guess a writer always wants a captive reader, no matter who!

It's so important to me to name what is real but also to reassure my children that I have the strength to face whatever is coming, just as they do. And while I'm actively working to accept that my life on earth will end much sooner than I ever imagined, I am still having difficulty understanding what my early death means in a daily way. How do I spend what limited time I have left? I once heard time described as a precious and nonrenewable resource. Damn. How much time I have wasted! How much I have spent staring at screens rather than into the faces of those I love the most! But also, what is there to do now but go gently with myself and vow to do it better tomorrow, for as many tomorrows as I get?

Our relationship with time is so curious to me now—how we assume we will have it, how we squander it, how we unknowingly numb ourselves to the gift of it. With limited energy and limited time, I'm asking myself where is it most important for me to focus my attention? I could justify centering on the past, because I want to capture my favorite memories, which are so precious to me. And I've considered obsessing over the future because I want to shore up anything helpful that I possibly can for Robbie and our kids. I feel simultaneously like I need quiet time alone, and to be surrounded by everyone I love the most, which is a lot of people! Like a woman about to give birth who asks to get quiet so she can find her strength for the great transition from one thing to the next, I feel I need the same as I approach my death. And in these times of quiet, I'm asking questions about both the past I have already lived and a future I can't yet see.

I want to remember the past and get my stories down so my children can know them and, in turn, know me and how I tried to live. I also want to reminisce with the people I love. I want to rehash old stories—let the snot come out of my nose a final time when I talk with Margo about eating that slice of pie she thought a kid ate, or with Laudie about Ben washing his dirty blacksmith's feet with her good face soap. Or that summer I practically lived with Dee, and my head itched all the time and she would patiently scratch it, and after eight weeks of constant itching, while sleeping in the same bed, directing camp together, traveling together, I finally confirmed I had head lice the whole time! And she never got it! When I scan my past, I see that I have been a constant seeker. My seeking has been relentlessly hopeful, and part of that hope includes an obligation to share what I have found along the way. Reminiscing about stories of my parents and brothers and cousins and grandparents and youth group helps me connect to a sense of wonder and gratitude for the life I have lived and for God's faithfulness and deep love every moment of my forty-one years. And I wonder, how can these things I've been through before help me now?

I am also thinking about the future constantly. I realize now that to marry or to become a parent is to hitch oneself to a future that is not and cannot be guaranteed. No part of an embodied future is guaranteed except for death. I think about everything I will miss, and what I won't be alive to witness or experience or endure or bounce back from. I think about specifics—no singing show tunes in the minivan. No burnt toast with butter in the mornings. No snuggling up to watch cooking shows. No walks together circling the neighborhood we love so much. Since I don't and can't know what happens in death for one who has died, I don't know if I can call this my loss or simply/not-so-simply theirs? Part of my focus on the future is my desire to make a smooth path for loved ones in a tangibly helpful way—printing family photos, revisiting our advanced directive documents, setting aside gifts to open on special occasions in the future, finally cleaning out the basement, and I don't know, ending misogyny in all forms!

Our friend David, who is a parent to similar-aged children as us and is a hospice chaplain, commented that my kids really aren't old enough to understand my death now. But what we can do now is give them the love and support and connection they will need to process my death in years to come. That helped me because I know I can love love love them and hold them and stay present to them now in ways that bring comfort and connection, but I cannot understand this myself, let alone explain it to them or make sense of it with them.

In my limited time left, what will deliver me from this pain and sorrow? There's an Indigo Girls song called "Our Deliverance" with a prescient lyric by Emily Saliers: "We may be looking for our deliverance, but it has already been sent." My interpretation of this song's meaning is that we obsess over an urgent preoccupation with something or someone to save us, and forget the truth that we're already delivered by the great mystery of God. There's a story in the Gospel of Thomas—which is one of the accounts of Jesus's life not included in the canon—in which a crowd is gathered around him and he says, "Y'all keep looking for the kingdom of God over here and over there, but don't you know the kingdom of God is in you and among you already?"

And there it is. I search and search for what has already found me—Love that is born of me, part of me, surrounding me, holding me. And it's this present and boundless Love who delivers us, and then never lets us go, never lets us go.

A Deep Yes

I recently woke up with an old Tracy Chapman song lyric in my mind—"And remember the tin man found he had what he thought he lacked." The words caught me in the night, as if its message were meant for me at exactly that moment, even as newly emerging losses mix me up and prevent me from engaging in what I love. But dammit if there aren't also newfound gifts in these losses, and as with any practice of gratitude, it helps me to notice them and name them.

One example from a week recently: Evenings typically feel overwhelming as we exhausted parents attempt to navigate as much normalcy as we can for Lulah and Thomas. And it was in fact my exhaustion and limitations one particular evening that resulted in one of the top-five nights of my entire life. While Robbie and Thomas played in the park across the street, Lulah made dinner for the two of us, all by herself. I sat on a stool at the counter and listened to her stories as she cooked. Without trying to pile on expectations about the meal or force the evening timeline and routine, I told her how lucky the boys are—and will be—to have her cooking amazing food for them and with them, and what a gift it will be for them to eat a little less of what I expect will be a lot of frozen pizza after I die. I honestly wish I could remember more specifics about the words we exchanged and the promises we made, but I think I was so focused on the moment and how much she made me laugh, and how good it felt to be part of that moment. I wanted to be present for her and present for myself and for what's possible still in my motherhood and in her personhood and still-burgeoning, still-becoming, still-so-tender, still needing a mom, and me still here to be it.

Limitations and loss offer us the invitation to find what we want but think we lack. In newly emerging losses we also find newly emerging gifts. This is not a new concept, or novel in any way. I remember when Robbie and I were first married and blending our modest finances, we assumed we didn't have enough money to take a weekly date night. But at our request, my mother-in-law helped us make our first budget, and we realized we could afford to go on dates! Who knew we could find such simple freedom in a budget—which, by most accounts, is something we perceive as a limitation?

I heard somewhere that we either find shelter or we become it. I mean, don't we all rest under trees someone else first planted? We want a place in the shade of that tree, where the protection and affirmation and rest we so desperately want reside. But we translate our limitations into stories that tell us we can't ever find it or don't deserve it or can't access it somehow. But losing something or someone invites a deep look-around and a look inward, and we find exactly what we think we lack.

I've been reflecting on how while Robbie and I belong to each other, he is not mine. And our children are not mine either. I have to remind myself that they were never mine. They belong to themselves and to the light and joy of God. And while they are not mine and cannot be mine, they can be shelter for me. In order to be shelter for myself and for our family, we sense we need to put more limits on our days and commitments. And part of establishing that, and receiving that, and protecting that, and even embracing the gifts in this shelter, is saying no to a lot more so we can say a deep yes to much less.

I am spending more and more time in bed, and while I cannot read, I feel so much gratitude for the sounds of the words and generous perspectives of friends and family through my headphones from emails and messages. It has meant so much to me and continues to mean so much to me to hear from so many—people I have known all my life, as well as people I have never met face-to-face. But the memories, the impressions, the hope, the humor—what a shelter every word of their writing and sharing continues to be for me. As these tumors hold court in my mind and mix me up in these sad and terrible ways, I find shelter in new thanks and new praise and in another day—and even in how healing these salty tears taste pouring into my open mouth as I wail my thanks for this unexpected, unbelievable, boundless shelter of love.

Gray Matter

Some of What it Might Be Like

Some of what it might be like:

It might be I'm a waxy leaf, rushing downstream, following the curve of the water, flipping, tumbling, somersaulting down the watershed, a delight in the water

Or a graceful and deep-throated pelican, joining its companions in a perfect *V* of flight, falling into formation, circling over our beloved Jekyll Island, dipping down for an early fish at the first pang of hunger

Or maybe I will be cosmic. A ball of light, a star in the night sky, obvious and out loud. Wayfinding, unapologetic, shooting

Or maybe I will be a song, golden words rolling off of someone's tongue, a tune anyone can hum. Or maybe I will be the ear who hears it

Or a sturdy stick, hewn by nature, the height of a man, found in the forest by some hiker needing a third leg of support. Not precious but perfect

Or as some tenacious perennial herb, comfrey maybe, driving its deep taproot into the soil, devoting my energy to making a flush of new dark leaves and purple blossoms, medicine for the earth

Or maybe a wide quilt, large enough to cover a multitude, made from cotton rags and worn denim, heavy and laid over a soldier terrified of war

Or a crop of corn, an old heirloom maize that has been saved and planted for centuries, dense nutrition for a whole community, and there is always enough

Or a box turtle, lounging on a log to get as much of that hot sun, patient to get my fill of heat, content to go slow, content with only what I need and nothing more

Or a feathery asparagus patch, spears pushing up stronger and thicker year over year, outrageous green beauty, order beneath chaos

Or maybe I will be the forest floor, sweet, damp, constantly renewing itself through death and decomposition

Maybe we become all of this and more

Acknowledgments

My desire is that these internal conversations that I've aired out on the pages here will in some ways show how grateful I feel to all of you, for being a part of this community of love that is so present with me. And the shelter that this book has become for me has been constructed by so many folks known and unknown to me. Thank you.

To my classmate, friend, and agent, Margaret Riley King. To our brilliant and patient editor Becky Nesbitt. To Leita and Sophie. To everyone else we didn't meet but who helped at Convergent, Random House, and William Morris.

To everyone at Vanderbilt, including Dr. Moots, Laura, Dr. Thompson, and Dr. Lola Chambliss.

To the Nashville Food Project, then and now.

To the Caring Bridge community that gave me so much support from the beginning.

To the Circle—you are everything to me.

To Sally for helping me with all the words early on.

To Margo and Laudie.

To my mom and dad, and Roy and Luke.

To Lulah and Thomas, I love you all the love.

And always and finally, to Robbie.

Notes

A LITTLE MORE TIME

1. Sharon Olds, interview by Krista Tippett, *On Being with Krista Tippett,* March 14, 2019, https://onbeing.org/programs/sharon-olds-odes-to-the -bleep/#transcript.

WATERMARK

1. David Whyte, *Consolations: The Solace, Nourishment and Underlying Meaning of Everyday Words* (Many Rivers Press, 2005), pp. 8–11.

ORDINARY RITUALS

1. Rumi, "A Great Wagon," *The Essential Rumi,* trans. Coleman Barks (Harper-SanFrancisco, 1995), p. 36.

GOING BACK TO GOD

1. Anita Barrows and Joanna Macy, trans., "Alles wird wieder groß sein und gewaltig," *Rilke's Book of Hours: Love Poems to God* (Riverhead Books, 2005), p. 121.

THAT HARD WAY

1. Adrienne Rich, *On Lies, Secrets, and Silence: Selected Prose 1966–1978* (W.W. Norton, 1979), p. 188.

THE SALMON

1. Stephen Mitchell, ed. and trans., "XXIX," *Ahead of All Parting: The Selected Poetry and Prose of Rainer Maria Rilke* (The Modern Library, 1995), p. 519.
2. Larkspur Conservation, https://larkspurconservation.org/.
3. Peace Prayer of Saint Francis, https://www.loyolapress.com/catholic-resources/prayer/traditional-catholic-prayers/saints-prayers/peace-prayer-of-saint-francis/.
4. Patrice Karst, *The Invisible String* (Little, Brown, 2018).

HALE, HALLOWED, HOLY

1. Wendell Berry, *The Art of the Commonplace: The Agrarian Essays of Wendell Berry* (Counterpoint, 2002), pp. 98–99.

NORMAL DAYS

1. Mary Jean Irion, "Let Me Hold You While I May," *Yes, World: A Mosaic of Meditation* (Richard Baron Publishing, 1970), p. 53.

AS IF

1. Maxine Kumin, *Always Beginning: Essays on a Life in Poetry* (Copper Canyon Press, 2000), p. 144.

Credits

About the Author

TALLU SCHUYLER QUINN was the founder of the Nashville Food Project, an organization that seeks to bring people together to grow, cook, and share nourishing food, cultivate community, and alleviate hunger. She earned a BFA in papermaking and bookbinding from the Appalachian Center for Craft and an MDiv from Union Theological Seminary at Columbia University, where she focused on ritual studies. Tallu made her home in Nashville with her husband, Robbie, and their daughter and son.

About the Artwork

The eight artworks sprinkled throughout the book are parts of projects that my kids and I did together. We used different media, with sponges, and potatoes, and lots of drippy brushes, to make them. As I was looking through all of my old art from the last three decades, from charcoal drawings done for my thesis in seminary to a bound book of papers made from local Tennessee plants, these pieces stood out to me because, as I turned my head to look at them within my remaining field of vision, they best captured how visually and cognitively confusing my experience is right now.